Behavioral Objectives

A GUIDE TO INDIVIDUALIZING LEARNING

Social Studies

JOHN C. FLANAGAN
ROBERT F. MAGER
WILLIAM M. SHANNER

Westinghouse Learning Press
Palo Alto, California

Division of Westinghouse Learning Corporation

Copyright © 1971 by Westinghouse Learning Corporation

Library of Congress Catalog Card Number: 72–149052

First Edition, Third Printing

Printed in the United States of America

contents

preface

A huge advantage of an instructional objective derives from the simple fact that it is written. Once it is written, it is visible. Once it is visible, it can be reviewed, evaluated, modified, and improved.

Objectives are frequently discussed but seldom seen. In these volumes you can see approximately four thousand instructional objectives in the subject areas of language arts, mathematics, science, and social studies ranging from grade one through grade twelve. This collection represents the cooperative efforts of over one hundred classroom teachers and an almost equal number of staff members at the American Institute for Research and Westinghouse Learning Corporation.

Since these volumes present written objectives rather than a discussion about objectives, they become the criteria by which materials are selected, content outlined, instructional procedures and educational technology developed, and tests and examinations prepared. All these aspects of an educational program are really the means for accomplishing the basic educational purpose.

This collection serves to stimulate teachers and educators in selecting and developing behavioral objectives for their own use. These objectives may be criticized and evaluated, revised and modified; objectives may be added or deleted, all with the purpose of arriving at an appropriate set of educational outcomes to meet the educational needs of a local situation and of individual students.

The rather obvious purpose of an instructional objective should be to make clear to teachers, students, and other interested persons what youngsters should be able to do as a result of the instructional program. A well-written instructional objective should specify under what conditions and to what extent a certain kind of student performance can be expected.

Unfortunately, school systems commonly lack a comprehensive and reasonably consistent set of educational objectives. Educational goals and objectives are frequently expressed only in broad, global terms, and the question of what and how to teach is left to a considerable extent to the teacher. As a result, quality in the schools is closely associated with the qualified and skillful teacher. No doubt considerable excellent educational work is done by artistic teachers who, while they may not have a clear conception of goals, do have an intuitive sense of good teaching. Their materials are significant, and they develop topics effectively with students. They clarify the educational objectives (even objectives not directly stated) through their actions as they teach intuitively.

If the foregoing were to serve as a basis for defining education, then the "intuitiveness of the artistic teacher" would have to be built into the educational program. This, of course, cannot be done. The alternative is to start with clearly defined, rather than implied, instructional objectives.

Educational objectives—even clearly stated, specific objectives—are, in the final analysis, matters of choice and thus are value judgments. The question then arises:

> Who provides these value judgments? In the last analysis, the public schools are operated to meet the needs of society. Some of the objectives, along with rules regarding who shall attend school, are provided for in state constitutions and by-laws. Other objectives are set forth by the efforts of elected representatives of the people of a community. Some are provided by professional educators hired to operate the schools. Still others come from our knowledge of children themselves and how they learn. All of these sources effectively furnish the educational objectives for a local public school. Objectives will change with the changing conditions of the times, sometimes quickly, as with Sputnik, but usually slowly.

In evaluating and summarizing instructional objectives, whatever their source, certain kinds of information and knowledge provide a more intelligent basis than others for making decisions about objectives. If certain facts are known and understood, the probability is increased that judgments about objectives will be wise and that educational goals will gain in significance, objectivity, and validity. For this reason the so-called scientific study of the curriculum has largely concerned itself with investigations that may provide a more adequate basis for wise selection of instructional objectives than has previously been available.

What sources can be used for acquiring information from which objectives can be derived? This question has been the subject of much controversy between essentialists and progressives, between

PREFACE

subject specialists and child psychologists, between sociologists and philosophers, between this school group and that school group.

Progressives and child psychologists emphasize the importance of studying the child to find out what kinds of interests he has, what problems he encounters, what purposes he has in mind. They see this information as providing the basic source for selecting objectives. Essentialists and subject specialists, on the other hand, are impressed by the large body of knowledge collected over many thousands of years, the so-called cultural heritage, and emphasize this body of knowledge as the primary source for deriving objectives. They view objectives as essentially the basic learnings selected from the vast cultural heritage of the past.

Many sociologists and others concerned with the pressing problems of contemporary society see in an analysis of today's world the basic information from which objectives can be derived. They view the school as the agency for helping young people to deal effectively with the critical problems of life in modern society. If existing problems can be determined, then, the sociologist feels, the objectives of the school are to provide the knowledge, skills, and attitudes that will help people to deal intelligently and effectively with contemporary problems. On the other hand, educational philosophers recognize that there are basic values in life, largely transmitted from one generation to another by means of education. They see the school as aiming essentially at the transmission of basic values derived by comprehensive philosophic study; hence they view educational philosophy as the source from which objectives can be derived.

The point of view recommended here is that no single source of information is adequate as a basis for wise and comprehensive decisions about the objectives of education. Each of the sources described has certain values to commend it. Each source should be given consideration in planning. In this way educational programs may be developed that are flexible and suitable for any specific public-school situation, regardless of whether that situation is influenced primarily by a single viewpoint or by a combination of attitudes concerning educational objectives.

Although the objectives in these volumes contribute to solving the difficult problem of delineating a curriculum, they should not be considered as a final and perfect product. Any set of objectives must in fact be considered tentative, requiring continuous updating and reevaluation to the educational purposes and programs at hand. To have critical comments made about one's objectives should be taken as a compliment, since criticism can only be made when one has given the thought and taken the time to write the objectives down.

In spite of the great effort and the number of man-hours that have gone into the task of compiling the objectives in these volumes, several of the objectives listed cannot yet be considered to be "true objectives," if by objectives we mean instructional outcomes described in terms of performance. In fact, the editors wish to make the following comments as to why some of the objectives herein are open to multiple interpretation.

1. Some objectives describe a classroom activity taking place during the process of learning, rather than the performance to be exhibited by the proficient student after learning.

2. Some objectives lack a description of, or even a suggestion for, the stimulus conditions under which a student is to perform. Conversely (and perversely), seemingly unimportant stimulus conditions are occasionally included.

3. Some statements (this term seems more appropriate here than objectives) fail to suggest any sort of criteria. Though not all objectives demand criteria, this lack makes for a certain vagueness in the phrasing of some objectives.

With slight editorial and organizational modifications, the objectives in these volumes are the objectives for Project PLAN. Project PLAN is a system of individualized education, operative at grades one through twelve in the subject areas of language arts, mathematics, science and social studies.

Project PLAN was conceived by Dr. John C. Flanagan, and to some extent evolved from the findings of Project TALENT, a large-scale, long-range project involving the collection of comprehensive information about education in the United States. Project TALENT involved the testing of a sample of 440,000 students in 1,353 secondary schools in all parts of the country in March 1960, with subsequent follow-up studies.

PREFACE

Through Dr. Flanagan's efforts, Project PLAN was brought into being in February 1967 as a joint effort of the American Institute for Research, Westinghouse Learning Corporation, and thirteen school districts.[1] Dr. Flanagan has continued to direct the developmental and research work on Project PLAN since that date. Assisting in the developmental work of Project PLAN has been Dr. Robert F. Mager, who is well known for his book *Preparing Instructional Objectives.*[2] Dr. Mager's philosophy was followed in the development of the objectives in these volumes.

The objectives in these volumes, then, have originated from teachers and have been tried out in schools. We wish to acknowledge the efforts of the teachers (their names are listed below) who were assigned by their school districts to work for a year at the American Institute for Research in Palo Alto. Without their contributions these volumes of objectives would not have been possible.

Archdiocese of San Francisco, Department of Education: Sister Maura Cole, Marian Bonnet, Janice Edminster, Sister Charlene Foster, Sister Bernice Heinz, Sister Patricia Hoffman, Sister Mary Vincent Gularte, Sister Anita Kelly, Sister Jeanne Marie Sosic

---

1. Archdiocese of San Francisco, Department of Education, San Francisco, California; Fremont Unified School District, Fremont, California; San Carlos Elementary School District, San Carlos, California; San Jose Unified School District, San Jose, California; Santa Clara Unified School District, Santa Clara, California; Sequoia Union High School District, Redwood City, California; Union Elementary School District, San Jose, California; Bethel Park School District, Bethel Park, Pennsylvania; Hicksville Public School District, Hicksville, New York; Penn Trafford School District, Harrison City, Pennsylvania; Pittsburgh Public Schools, Pittsburgh, Pennsylvania; Quincy Public Schools, Quincy, Massachusetts; Wood County Schools, Parkersburg, West Virginia.
2. R. F. Mager, *Preparing Instructional Objectives* (Palo Alto, Calif.: Fearon Publishers, 1962). The cooperating school districts furnished classroom teachers each year from 1967 through June 1970 to develop the objectives and to prepare the Teaching-Learning Units that enable students to accomplish the objectives. These teachers worked under the supervision of American Institute for Research and Westinghouse Learning Corporation professional personnel. The director of these activities was Dr. William M. Shanner. At the end of each year the teachers returned to their respective school districts to initiate the instructional programs organized from the objectives.

PREFACE

Bethel Park School District: Lora Moroni, Gordon Lepri, James Johnson, Judith Andrews, Flora Belle Faddis, David Loadman, Mary Lou Ertman, Roger Johnson, Robert N. Manson, Anna Marie Kerlin, Frances Chase, Robert M. Caldwell

Fremont Unified School District: Lyndall Sargent, Gail Pagan, Rex W. Estes, Caroline Breedlove, Monique Lowy, Charles Swanson, Eileen Trefz, Robert Fairlee, Beverly Ulbricht, Forrest W. Dobbs, Roy C. Fields, Bertram K. Robarts

Hicksville Public School District: Elayne Kabakoff, Richard C. Leuci, Terrence Boylan, Janet Findlay, Willard Prince, Edward Albert, Phyllis A. Kabakoff, Lawrence Dauch, Gerald Shanley, Marjorie Giannelli, Tom Bannan, Gerard F. Irwin

Hughson Union High School District: Warren Green

Penn-Trafford School District: Gary Fresch, Mary Ann Kovaly, Michael Demko, Jack Reilly, Victor Bohince, David Garvin, La-Velle Hirshberg, R. Bruce Robinson

Pittsburgh Public Schools: Ann Mulroy, Jean Brooke, Kenneth Fraser, Shirley Fullerton, Ruth Aaron, Donald Coudriet, Cecilia Sukits, Carmen Violi, Samuel D. Martin, Paul J. Schafer, Mary South, Patricia Sellars

Quincy Public Schools: Jean Ann MacLean, Priscilla A. Dauphinee, Francis Keegan, Katherine Norris, Dennis Carini, Richard Russell, Stephen Fishman, Jack K. Merrill, Marcia A. Mitchell, Robert J. Mattsson, Margaret E. Flynn

San Carlos Elementary School District: Helen Dodds, Natalie Klock, Edith Bryant, Maxine Ross, Elizabeth Movinski, Martha A. Elmore, Charles B. Whitlock, Betty Lee, Lee G. Jensen

San Jose Unified School District: Allaire Bryant, Rise Berry, Hal Garrett, Kathy Roberts, William Harvel, Judy Opfer, Judi Wells, Don Crowell, Oran T. Adams, Marilyn D. Johnson, Alice S. Anderson, Sylvia Atallah

Santa Clara Unified School District: Nancy Wylde, Ruth Hessenflow, Arthur A. Hiatt, Herman Neufeld

PREFACE

Sequoia Union High School District: Gale Randall, Rex Fortune, Robert W. DuBois

Union School District: Jo Ann Risko, Peggy Schwartz, Rose Yamasaki, Glenn Moseley, Sue Coffin, Tod Hodgdon, Barbara S. Donley, Frank Kelly

Wood County Schools: Roberta Adkins, Mary Rector, Larry Myers, Virginia Haller, John Hoyes, Connie Chapman, Ada Ardelia Price, David V. Westfall, Nancy M. Rice, John W. Apgar

In addition, the contributions of the following persons should be acknowledged. Mary June Erickson, language arts; Josephine J. Matthews, Dr. Marie Goldstein, and Dr. Gordon McLeod, mathematics; Marvin D. Patterson, science; Dr. Vincent N. Campbell, social studies; Sarah M. Russell, primary; Katheryn K. Woodley, Dr. Mary B. Willis, Debbra D. Michaels, performance standards; and Dr. Helen D. Dell, editorial

Final acknowledgment should go to those who use the objectives in these volumes. Objectives alone, an educational program do not make. They provide at best only a framework. The responsibility for the learning must rest on the student, guided by the teacher, and supervised by the school administration.

William M. Shanner

Palo Alto, California
December 15, 1970

INTRODUCTION

Although these volumes are mainly self-explanatory, the reader may find helpful the information that follows. The organization of the objectives is discussed, terms are defined, and the numbering system is clarified.

When a text is made up of many small parts, the constraints of print mean that each item has a fixed position on a page and within a volume, a position that establishes a sequential relationship with all preceding and following items regardless of whether such a relationship is logical or intentional. Since behavioral objectives may potentially be arranged in so many ways, it is important to understand how this collection is arranged and organized to avoid any unwarranted assumption that a prescriptive sequence is being suggested.

The objectives have been organized into four volumes, based on a natural, though often overlapping, grouping of the four major subject areas: language arts, social studies, mathematics, and science. Each volume ranges from Grade 1 through Grade 12. This arrangement is based on the needs of teachers and curriculum designers to perceive the span of a particular subject over the school years. An equally good argument can be made for presenting all the material across subjects for a single age level in one volume to emphasize the interrelatedness of the disciplines. The drawback of this format lies in the wide variations of curricula chosen in different local situations for a given age group. Subject-focused volumes, therefore, seem to be the most useful, with cross-referencing and cross-indexing to relate the subject areas.

Although each volume covers the traditional period from Grade 1 through Grade 12, grouping of objectives into single grade levels is inappropriate, again because of the flexibility of modern curriculum design. Instead, the objectives within each volume have been grouped according to Primary, Intermediate, and Secondary levels. The objectives in these groups overlap to some extent, but use of the three designations divides the objectives into sections of manageable size.

SOCIAL STUDIES

These three groups, or levels, may be roughly defined as follows:

Primary: Primary refers to Grades 1 through 3 and covers the material that, in most cases, is presented in these three years. Some readiness material is included that covers preschool years. The more advanced material may be applicable to the Intermediate level; some objectives from the Intermediate level may be appropriate for late Primary.

Intermediate: Intermediate refers to the years usually included in Grades 4 through 8. Once again, this decision is arbitrary; curricula for Grades 7 and 8 are sometimes closely related to high-school studies. Where a junior high school includes Grades 7, 8, and 9, the Intermediate and the Secondary objectives need to be considered selectively.

Secondary: Secondary designates high school, from freshman through senior years. The material presumes that the student has covered the work included in the earlier grades. There is little or no re-presentation of review topics, nor are there objectives designed for remedial work.

Within subject areas there are many ways to subdivide material. It is important to have enough subdivisions to be meaningful and yet not so many that overlapping and confusion result.

The following lists show the topics selected for each volume.

LANGUAGE ARTS
  Listening Skills
  Speaking Skills
  Reading Skills
  Writing Skills
  Grammar Skills
  Study Skills
  Personal Communication and Development Skills
  History and Dialectology
  Classification, Interpretation, and Analysis of Literary Forms
  Original Writing
  Oral and Dramatic Interpretation
  Critical Analysis of Media

PRIMARY

HISTOry

SS 005 Show your understanding of changes in communities and reasons for them.   II

Describe changes in your neighborhood that you can remember (i.e., natural disasters, new discoveries, businesses moving, new uses of land, inventions, families moving, construction of different kinds of buildings, people working as a group on a problem).   II

Identify five factors that help to make a neighborhood change.   I

Identify factors in the natural environment of your community that made it possible for man in early days to live where your community is now located.   I

Given pictures, films, and stories about life in your community long ago, compare and contrast various activities in the history of your community with activities in the earliest Indian community and in the early settlers' community.   VI

Describe changes that have taken place in one of the following kinds of communities: desert, rain forest, grassland, or arctic.   II

Explain reasons for changes in one of the particular kinds of communities you have studied.   II (SS 020)

Tell whether the changes in a particular kind of community might be considered advantages or disadvantages from the point of view of people who live there.   IV (SS 020)

Contrast the various ways that desert people have retained ancient traditions and customs with the ways that they have adapted to modern life.   VI (SS 020)

Given a list of some early contributions of desert people to the world, describe how man uses three of these contributions today.   II

Given a list of sentences, identify each sentence as one that tells about life in a primitive community or as one that tells about life in a modern community.   I

SOCIAL STUDIES

PRIMARY

SOCIOLOGY and anTHropOLOGY

SS 010 Show your understanding of the interdependence of people in families. II

Classify family members as "nuclear family" or "extended family." ("Nuclear family" includes mother, father, son, daughter, and baby; "extended family" includes cousins, aunts, uncles, grandmothers, grandfathers.) II

Through role-playing, present at least two roles that each member of the family usually plays in the normal routine of family life. III (LA 196)

On a globe, locate areas where Lapps and Eskimos live. Explain why it has been necessary for these peoples to have close family ties. II (SS 040, SS 075)

SS 015 Show your understanding of types of neighborhoods. II

Tell where children can meet other children in a neighborhood. I

Identify kinds of public services (transportation, business, recreation and housing facilities) that most small-town neighborhoods have. I

Make a map of your school neighborhood. Put as many streets, houses, parks, schools, and buildings as you can on your map. III (SS 045)

Tell two traits about city people, and name two kinds of city buildings, two kinds of city transportation, and two kinds of city noises. I

List facts about suburban neighborhoods. I

Explain the differences between city life and rural life. II

Tell how life in a suburb differs from life in small towns and from cities. II

2

PRIMARY

Tell about transportation, houses, food, and neighbors in farm neighborhoods. I

Explain what people like about living in small towns, cities, suburbs, or rural areas. II

SS 020 Show your understanding of types of communities and their characteristic customs. II

Given a list of questions, identify the questions that would be important to ask if you wanted to find out what a community is like. I (SS 170)

Classify descriptions of community environments as cultural or natural. II (SC 025)

Describe one custom that is unique to communities in each of the following areas: desert, rain forest, arctic, mountain, grassland, or seacoast. II

Describe similarities and differences in customs (social and cultural) and in ways of adapting to the environment (including satisfaction of basic needs) in three of the following environments: desert, arctic, tropical rain forest, mountain, or grassland. II

Recognize two examples of customs that are different for people living in two given communities with very similar natural environments (for example: mountain, desert, grassland, seacoast, rain forest, or arctic). II

From the following topographical areas, choose one in which to plan a community: desert, mountain, seacoast, grassland. Describe the advantages and disadvantages of settling in this particular environment. II (SS 080, SS 175)

Predict some customs and values that might exist among the people living in your planned community, and discuss which of these should be considered in the planning. III

Given a list of statements about the environments of communities, classify them as belonging to the natural or the cultural environment of the community. II (SS 060)

Define *natural resources*. From a list, identify things that are or are not natural resources. II

SOCIAL STUDIES

Given a list of some features of a community, identify physical features and cultural features. II (SC 025)

Given a chart showing five areas of a community and a list of items descriptive of each area, classify the items most common to each area. Explain why residential and commercial sections were not so separate in earlier cities as they are in modern cities. IV

SS 025 Show your understanding of the interdependence of people in communities. II

Tell things that are important and things that are not important when you make friends. I (SS 175)

Explain what you are learning in school that will help you share ideas. II (SS 175)

Describe what you think makes a good neighbor. II

Given pictures of neighborhood workers, identify pictures of neighborhood *volunteer* workers. I

Explain how residential and commercial areas of a community depend upon each other. II

Explain why people who have come from other countries are important in cities. II

Name some things that a tribe could do for a person that the person alone could not do so well. I

Identify reasons that people have for living in the following kinds of communities rather than alone: mountain, rain forest, desert. I

SS 030 Show your understanding of the interdependence of communities. II

Report to the class two examples of ways your community depends upon other communities. Include samples or pictures of products or services from other communities. II (SS 055)

Explain why developed grassland communities and urban communities are dependent upon each other. II (SS 065)

PRIMARY

Predict what the consequences would be for a grassland community and an urban community if all contact stopped between the two groups.   III (SS 080)

Suggest one way in which the United Nations could help a mountain community.   II

POLITICAL SCIENCE

SS 035   Show that you know some factors involved in the process of government.   I

List at least two activities in an election.   I

From pictures or phrases, identify services provided by government.   I

Make a list of things that would happen if people stopped paying taxes.   I

Pretend that children in your school are frequently injured while playing in the school yard at recess. Make a list of ways to solve this problem and decide on the best one.   VI (SS 185)

On a map find the capital of your state and the capital of the United States.   I (SS 180)

Identify needs filled by government in your own community (for example: police and fire protection, recreation, mail and sanitation services, environment control).   I (SS 025)

GEOGRAPHY

SS 040   Show that you can locate and identify places, climatic regions, and physical features on maps and globes.   III (SS 180)

On a map or globe, locate and identify the land masses called continents.   I

Locate and name the major oceans on a map or globe.   I

On a topographic map or globe, locate desert areas on the following continents: Africa, Asia, North America, and Australia.   I

5

Locate and name the hemispheres on a globe: northern, southern, eastern, and western.   I

Locate and identify the two polar regions and the equator on a globe.   I

SS 045   Show that you can use map symbols and judge distances on maps.   III (SS 180)

Locate the directions north, east, south, and west on a map.   I

Match given map symbols with the pictures or words they represent.   I

Make a map of a local area such as your classroom or your school neighborhood.   III (SS 015)

Make a map from a picture of a farm.   III

From a map, indicate the distance between two given points.   III

Recognize distortions on a world map.   II

On a relief map, locate common land forms (mountains, hills, islands, and plains) and common water forms (rivers and lakes) by interpreting color or symbols.   II

SS 050   Show that you can relate physical features to climatic regions on maps and globes.   III

Starting from the equator, locate on a map or globe the regions of the earth that have the hottest and coldest climates.   I (SS 080)

Tell the similarities in location, climate, and vegetation among rain forest areas of the Congo, the Amazon, and southeast Asia.   I (SS 080)

Name similarities in location, climate, and vegetation among the grassland areas of the world.   I (SS 065)

PRIMARY

Name and locate two major mountain ranges, and tell how these mountain ranges affect the climate, the rainfall, and the vegetation of surrounding areas. I (SS 060)

Match given climatic conditions with the following environments: desert, rain forest, arctic, mountain, grassland. I (SS 080)

SS 055 Show your understanding of relationships between environmental resources and human activities in your community. II

Identify and list ways that modern man changes or interacts with the natural environment of the following communities to serve his needs better: your community, a mountain community. I

Identify and list resources in the natural environment of your community that made it possible for man in early days to live where your community is now located. I (SS 005)

SS 060 Show your understanding of relationships between environmental resources and human activities in mountain regions. II

Explain why some mountain regions have large cities and why some do not. Give examples of mountain regions that have large cities and of those that do not. II

Explain why people in some mountain regions are engaged in mining or manufacturing while people in others are not. II (SS 145)

Include in your explanation the conditions necessary for successful manufacturing. II

Describe typical economic activities in rural mountain environments and in urban settings. II

SS 065 Show your understanding of relationships between environmental resources and human activities in grassland areas. II (SS 150)

Given a list of grazing animals, identify grazing animals of the developed grassland areas and grazing animals of the undeveloped grassland areas. Tell how these animals are used in each kind of area. I

Describe problems of particular concern to people who are directly involved in making a living in developed grassland areas, and problems of concern to people making a living in undeveloped grassland areas. II

Explain why the most densely populated areas of the world today were once grassland areas. II (SS 005)

SS 070 Show your understanding of relationships between environmental resources and human activities in desert communities. II

Describe the natural characteristics of two different desert communities. Describe how nomadic and settled groups have adapted differently to natural desert environments. II

SS 075 Show your understanding of relationships between environmental resources and human activities in arctic areas. II (SC 025)

Describe how arctic life is influenced by seasonal changes in the natural environment. II

Describe ways in which the Laplander uses the reindeer. Explain why the reindeer is so important. II

Explain how changes that are taking place in the Arctic are both advantageous and disadvantageous from the point of view of people who live there. II (SS 005)

Using a picture or a story, demonstrate how the arctic environment and man's ways of meeting his needs there are changing. III (SS 005, LA 030)

SS 080 Show your understanding of general effects of relationships between environmental resources and human activities. II (SC 025)

Explain why developed grassland communities and urban communities are dependent upon each other. II (SS 030)

8

PRIMARY

Predict what the consequences would be for a grassland community and an urban community if all contact stopped between the two groups.   III (SS 030)

Describe one custom that is unique to communities in each of the following areas: desert, rain forest, arctic, mountain, grassland.   II (SS 020)

Describe similarities and differences in the customs (social and cultural) and ways of adapting to the environment (including the basic needs) in three of the following environments: desert, arctic, tropical rain forest, mountain, or grassland.   II (SS 020)

Recognize two examples of customs that are different for people living in two given communities with very similar natural environments.   II (SS 020, SC 025)

From the following topographical areas, choose one in which to plan a community: desert, mountain, seacoast, grassland. Describe the advantages and disadvantages of settling in this particular environment.   II (SS 040)

Predict some customs and values that might exist among the people who live in your planned community. Discuss which of these customs should be considered in the planning.   III (SS 175)

Predict which living habits would continue to be useful and which habits would become useless or even harmful if a person moved from one community to another of the following types of communities: desert, arctic, tropical rain forest, mountain, or grassland.   III (SC 025)

economics

SS 085   Show that you understand the nature of basic human needs.   II

Given a set of pictures, recognize things that families must have (i.e., food, clothing, shelter).   II

Given a list or set of pictures, arrange items in the order you would obtain them, based on their necessity to life.   II

Tell how families are the same around the world in meeting the need for food, water, clothing, and shelter. I (SS 020)

Tell how families around the world are different in meeting basic needs. Include desert people and natives of tropical rain forests. I (SS 080)

Given a list of needs, identify basic physical needs of man and basic social needs of man. I

SS 090 Show your understanding of human dietary needs and of human activities concerned with meeting these needs. II

Describe how food is obtained today (i.e., fishing, hunting, growing, buying) and how primitive man got his food. Draw or paint pictures showing primitive man and contemporary man getting food. II (SS 005)

Identify each of these kinds of food: (1) dairy products, (2) meats, (3) grains, (4) vegetables, and (5) fruits. I

Name three products of the dairy, the bakery, or the truck farm. I

Identify foods that make a good breakfast, lunch, or dinner. I (SC 025)

Given a list of foods, select foods that would make a well-balanced diet. I (SC 025)

Given a set of pictures showing supermarket helpers, write a report describing how one of the helpers aids us in getting our food. III (LA 105, SS 175)

Tell what each of the following classes of food does for the human body: proteins, energy foods, vitamins, and minerals. I (SC 025)

From a list, classify foods into three groups: energy, protein, vitamins, and minerals. II (SC 025)

SS 095 Show that you know about various aspects of food processing. I

Tell the various ways we preserve food. I

PRIMARY

After conducting an experiment in preserving food, describe the steps used to preserve one kind of food. II

Show, in pictures or a story, at least three things you noticed after visiting a processing plant (ice cream, milk, bakery) or after seeing a movie of such a plant. II (LA 025, SS 175)

SS 100   Show that you know about various aspects of clothing and its production. I

Tell what makes up cloth. I

Classify fabrics (such as wool, silk, etc.) by fabric name and by texture. II

Name items of clothing made of each fabric, and match items named. I

Identify the sources of wool, silk, cotton, nylon, rayon, and linen. I

Explain, in order, the steps of making wool into cloth. II

Explain, in order, the steps of making silk into cloth. II

Identify materials used by a clothesmaker. Name five steps involved in the making of clothes. I

Make and label collections of samples of cloth from animal sources, from plant sources, and from sources of man-made fiber. III

By weaving paper, demonstrate how fibers are woven to make cloth. III

SS 105   Show your understanding of human needs for shelter and special adaptations to various conditions.   II (SC 025)

Draw pictures of rooms in a house. Match models of furniture to the rooms. III

Describe at least six types of shelter around the world. Construct a log cabin or igloo. III

SOCIAL STUDIES

SS 110 Show that you know about various aspects of building construction. I

Name various materials that are needed to construct buildings today. I

Explain why certain buildings in your neighborhood have exteriors made of wood, brick, concrete, plaster, glass, and steel. II (SS 015)

Explain what happens to a tree from the time it is a seed until it is turned into lumber. II (SC 025)

SS 115 Show your understanding of some aspects of trading and the use of money. II (MA 060)

Tell the meaning of barter. Tell the two conditions that are necessary before bartering can take place. Name items people used for barter in very early times. I

Tell items used for money before metal was used. I

Tell how coined money came to be used instead of earlier means of exchange and why it was an improvement. Tell one disadvantage of using coined money exclusively. I

Tell why paper money, as well as coined money, is used today. Tell how the government of a country controls the use of paper money. I

Predict what would happen if the flow of money suddenly stopped and no one could obtain currency. III

SS 120 Show your understanding of community service work. II

Name at least three community helpers. I

Present a written and/or oral report about a community helper. III (LA 195, SS 175)

Given pictures of neighborhood workers, identify pictures of neighborhood *volunteer* workers. I

PRIMARY

Given pictures of workers, describe what each worker is doing, and explain how his job helps the people in his neighborhood.   II

Identify an example of work that fulfills social needs of a community.   I (SS 025)

SS 125   Show that you know about workers and occupations that affect you.   I (SS 025)

From pictures or job titles, identify people who are producers of goods.   I

From pictures or job titles, identify people who are producers of services.   I

From pictures or job titles, identify people who are consumers of goods and services.   I

Classify the different kinds of work that people do into "jobs" or "occupations" (e.g., people who distribute letters have the occupational title of "mailman").   II

Tell what jobs or occupations people have in factories.   I

Participate in a group pantomime of occupations in a factory.   III (LA 196)

Name five jobs that must be done to produce a television news program. Name or suggest occupational titles for these jobs.   II

Given one example, explain how occupations differ in the amount of pay workers receive.   II (SS 115)

Present through pictures, a description, a skit, or by other means, aspects of an occupation that interests you.   III (LA 030, SS 165, SS 175)

SS 130   Show that you know about various aspects of merchandising.   I

Demonstrate that you recognize different kinds of stores by collecting pictures of a variety of stores, by drawing pictures, or by constructing models.   III

Name one thing you can get from a store that you cannot make because you do not have the skill.   I

Explain why stores advertise.   II

Participate in a classroom swap shop. Have one member of the class keep records of transactions to demonstrate what store owners must consider to make the most sales.   III (MA 060)

SS 135   Show that you can identify types of communication services. III (LA 145, LA 150)

Tell your address (house number, street, city, state) and telephone number.   I

Present a report about one machine that helps us to communicate. III (SS 175)

Describe systems that help people to communicate long distances (e.g., telephone, telegraph, postal service, communication satellites, etc.).   II

Name three examples of mass media.   I

Name five sections that can be found in a newspaper.   I

Explain what different kinds of information you can get from watching television.   II

Demonstrate that you understand the kinds of news information presented on television by performing a short skit for your class in which people play the parts of a television sponsor, a news commentator, and an interviewer.   III (LA 196)

SS 140   Show that you know about types of transportation services.   I

Identify modes of transportation and suggest other possible types (ship, car, bus, truck, airplane, train, animal, sled, ice skates, space vehicle).   I

PRIMARY

From a set of pictures, identify the ones that show how people travel from the suburbs to the city.   I

SS 145   Show that you know about various aspects of industrial production in factories.   I

Name one example of a factory product.   I

Describe what general kinds of materials are needed by a factory to produce a given product.   II

Having visited a factory, read a story about a factory, or seen a film about a factory, explain what you learned about making a product.   II (LA 025, SS 170)

Explain what decisions about money are needed to keep a factory going.   II (SS 115)

Tell two advantages and two disadvantages of having factories in a neighborhood.   I (SS 015)

Explain one reason why some factories have moved from the city to the suburbs.   II

SS 150   Show that you know about various aspects of farm production.   I

Name four different kinds of farms.   I

Describe things that help farmers produce more goods.   II

PSYCHOLOGY and PHILOSOPHY

SS 155   Show that you understand various basic aspects of communication.   II

Without using words, communicate to a friend. Be able to show your teacher how you communicated and what you communicated.   III (LA 196)

Tell some ways to communicate by using symbols of communication (e.g., globe, signal flags on a ship, traffic signal, skull and crossbones, map symbols, etc.). I

List as many ways to communicate as you can. I

Say "hello" in three different languages. I

SS 160 Show that you can apply problem-solving skills to personal problems. III (SS 185)

Name five steps in problem solving. I

Given a personal problem, suggest a way to solve it. II

SS 165 Show that you can make choices on the basis of needs, resources, and desires. III

Tell the difference between wanting and needing. Explain how financial resources can affect wants and needs. II

SOCIAL STUDIES INQUIRY SKILLS

SS 170 Show that you can make a list of questions to find out information. III

SS 175 Show that you can use information to make a short simple report orally, in pictures, or in writing. III

SS 180 Show that you can use maps and globes to locate places and to identify physical features, to judge distances, and to represent an area you know (your yard, neighborhood, or classroom). III

SS 185 Show that you understand the steps in problem solving and can apply them in dealing with your personal problems. III

INTERMEDIATE

History

SS 200 **Show that you can discuss the reasons that Europeans and, later, people from other parts of the world settled in North America, as well as the problems they encountered.   III**

From a list of reasons why Europeans came to America, identify one goal that was not realized immediately and tell why it was not.   I

Discuss examples of people who left Europe to go to the Americas before 1800 for each of the following reasons: religious, economic, and social.   III

Given a list of statements on colonization, classify them according to the advantages and disadvantages for (1) the mother country, (2) the colonists, and (3) the natives.   II

Recognize problems of colonizing the New World that all Europeans experienced.   II

Identify three reasons why American explorers and settlers first came to the following territories: Kentucky, Louisiana Territory, Texas, and California.   I

Given a number of events describing how the Louisiana Territory, Texas, or California was added to the United States, put the events in chronological order.   I

Identify one reason for the migration to North America of each of the following groups: Africans, Cubans, Eastern Europeans, English, Eskimos, French, German, Indians, Irish, Italians, Mexicans, Orientals, Puerto Ricans, Scandinavians, and Spanish.   I

SS 205 **Show your understanding of cultural and economic aspects of life in early America.   II (SS 245)**

Explain how tobacco enabled the colony of Virginia to survive economically.   II (SS 375)

From a list of crafts that were common in early settlements, describe how the people used their skills to meet their needs and the needs of others.   II (SS 250)

SOCIAL STUDIES

INTERMEDIATE

Explain how the historical restoration of a community can lead to knowledge about past events, achievements, and customs. Explain why the way of life in a historical community was different from ours today.   II (SS 245)

Given a description of colonial education, recognize the parts that do not describe education in most places today.   II (SS 255)

Given an activity that in colonial times was considered work and is looked upon today as recreation, explain the reasons for this change.   II

Describe briefly the life style (including types of food, transportation, housing, customs, and religious practices) of an early culture that existed in the area that now includes your state.   II

SS 210   On the basis of human goals and needs, make judgments about the events that led to the American Revolution. Consider the issues from the viewpoints of the English and of the American colonists.   VI

Explain why strife developed between the Indians and the English.   II (SS 260)

Explain why the colonists became dissatisfied with English rule.   II (SS 300)

Identify the major factors that contributed to the colonial desire for autonomy.   I

Empathizing with either the rebel or the Royalist (Tory) points of view and values concerning colonial differences with England, discuss how you (as a rebel or as a Royalist) feel about a given issue.   III (SS 420)

From brief descriptions of historical events, recognize events that reflect England's colonial attitude of mercantilism, such as her right to tax colonies and her right to organize her expanded colonies.   II (SS 370)

18

INTERMEDIATE

Explain the relationship between the English colonies and the mother country (later the United States and Great Britain) as reflected in their attitudes toward each other's use of the English language during each of the 17th, the 18th, the 19th, and the 20th centuries. II (LA 370)

Read the Declaration of Independence and translate it into terms that are meaningful and understandable to a classmate. II (SS 330)

Suggest three ways in which colonial cities contributed to causes of the American Revolution. II

Given the details of a significant American historical event in the colonial period, summarize in a brief written statement the major issues of the event. II (LA 255)

List British and American conditions in 1775 that could have influenced the outcome of the Revolutionary War. I

Read an article or outline describing a historical event. Given a list of causes, suggest the probable immediate cause of that event. II (LA 335)

Read an article or outline giving details of a historical event. Given a list of effects, predict the possible direct effects of that event. III (LA 335)

SS 215 **Show your understanding of the following aspects of your state's history by describing them: (1) culture, (2) natural environment, (3) industrial development, (4) government services, and (5) social problems. II (SS 330)**

Describe briefly the life style (including type of food, transportation, housing, customs, and religious practices) of an early culture that existed in the area that now includes your state. II (SS 245)

Explain when and why various ethnic groups settled in the city or area where you live. II (SS 260)

SOCIAL STUDIES

Recognize evidence of the influence that at least five foreign cultures brought to your community, such as manufactured products, architectural designs, foods, clothing styles, music, religion, etc. II

Describe your state in terms of its major landforms, climate, and natural resources, and locate the state on an unmarked map of North America. II (SS 350)

Explain two problems concerning the natural environment of your state. II (SS 365)

Identify several kinds of products and services in which your state specializes. I (SS 355)

Predict where manufacturing might be carried on in your state on the basis of the location of transportation routes and of raw materials. III (SS 370)

By locating centers of industry on a map and designating the center of population, demonstrate how industry (manufacturing, agriculture, and services) influences population distribution in your state. III (SS 335)

List two examples of how people in two distinct areas of your state serve each other's needs. I

Describe how the government of your state is organized. II (SS 330)

Describe a social problem that has occurred in your state as the result of change. II

Describe how two significant events in the history of your state have affected the subsequent development of the state. II

SS 220   Find information on a topic of your own choice concerning the War Between the States. II (SS 425)

INTERMEDIATE

Using any reference materials available, find out how differences between the North and the South in population and economy affected the development of sectionalism from 1800 to 1860.   III

Prepare and present a credible argument to support a given viewpoint on a specific issue during antebellum days in which Northern and Southern viewpoints differed. Your argument must be based on fact, and you must listen to and respond to the opposing viewpoint.   III (LA 230)

Identify major problems created by the Civil War, including specific burdens on civilians, problems faced by a typical soldier, and military problems faced by both sides.   I (SS 425)

Explain how the location of key cities affected the outcome of the Civil War.   II (SS 335)

SS 225   Show your understanding of settlement patterns by describing the settlement of two cities in terms of reasons for the locations.   II (SS 350)

On an outline map of the United States, locate the first major cities west of the Appalachian Mountains and identify a main reason for the development of each from a wilderness outpost to a city.   I (SS 350)

Discuss reasons for the origin of cities.   III (SS 370)

SS 230   Show your understanding of urban growth patterns by describing the growth of two cities in terms of (1) the industries that led to rapid growth, and (2) the unique characteristics of each city.   II

Find information on the origin and urban development of Seattle, San Francisco, Los Angeles, Salt Lake City, or Denver. Write a report on your findings, citing the sources.   III (LA 345)

Explain the relationship between factors of settlement, occupations of people, topography, etc., and the formation of cities in the South.   II (SS 350)

SOCIAL STUDIES

Analyze statements concerning the purpose for cities, inferring the writer's bias.   IV (SS 425)

Explain why the development of industries is a main cause of urbanization.   II (SS 370)

Prepare and present a research project in which you have studied the effects of the railroad on the urbanization of a particular city or region.   III (SS 370)

Describe how changes in the transportation of goods and people helped encourage the growth of the urban frontier.   II

Describe the social, political, and economic systems that made the colonial cities of Boston, Providence, Newport, New York, Philadelphia, and Charleston unique.   II (SS 290)

Identify contributions of such men as Benjamin Franklin to the improvement of city life.   I

Explain the effect of the Civil War on the growth of American cities.   II (SS 220)

Explain why the population of cities grew more than the population of rural America in the decades following the Civil War.   II (SS 245)

Identify reasons why immigrants came to American cities in the decades following the Civil War.   I (SS 225)

Describe ways that the inventions of the bridge, the trolley, and the subway have improved transportation in the cities.   II (SS 250)

Describe the urban problem that was reduced by each of the following technological developments: hydrants, concrete buildings, telephones, subways, water filters, automatic sprinklers, sewage disposals, incinerators, burglar alarm systems.   II (SS 250)

INTERMEDIATE

Differentiate the architectural pattern of urban structures that emphasize economic, practical values from the pattern of those that emphasize aesthetic or artistic values, using evidence from respected sources of information.   III (SS 255)

Make models or drawings illustrating ideas and new designs that have been advanced to improve and change cities.   III

Describe the growth of a large city in your state in terms of development of business, industry, agriculture, education and recreational facilities, and political-social organizations.   II

Recognize descriptions of different kinds of urban development patterns.   II (SS 225)

Identify the activities that take place in each of the following kinds of urban zones: (1) the central business district, (2) a zone in transition, and (3) a new residential suburb.   I (SS 370)

Explain, giving reasons and evidence, how social change is related to migration patterns into the urban areas.   II (SS 225)

List the opportunities for living and working you would expect to find in a city.   I (SS 410)

Describe at least one poverty program that is presently being implemented in an urban area of your state.   II (SS 310)

Find information that supports conclusions about the reasons for riots in American cities during the past decade.   III (SS 310, SS 425)

Write a response to the following question: Have American cities helped to unite (integrate) nonwhite and white Americans as they helped the immigrant groups earlier in our history?   III (SS 430)

Identify problems and opportunities that the immigrant faces today in coming to an American city.   I

Find information on programs designed to solve urban problems. III (LA 330)

Predict the consequences that may result from the expansion of densely populated urban areas. III

Suggest three areas in the United States that will be megalopolises by the year 2000 and explain why this will occur. II (LA 260)

Develop ideas from new designs proposed by city planning commissions into a plan for alleviating the traffic problems in cities. V (SS 430)

Discuss the effects of urban development patterns on given social groups and suggest causes for patterns of deviant behavior. Locate evidence from social research. III (SS 395)

Discuss this statement: "The city has served a 'melting pot' function in regard to immigrants." III

SS 235 Show that you can prepare and present a report showing how urban problems in the last half of the 19th century compare with urban problems of today. III (SS 430)

Identify reasons why immigrants came to American cities in the decades following the Civil War. I (SS 225)

List at least three problems common to European immigrants to the United States in the last half of the 19th century. I (SS 200)

Describe problems that laborers faced in American cities during the second half of the 19th century. II (SS 200)

Describe problems of city governments in the latter half of the 19th century. Include major urban problems such as fire, slums, pollution, and congestion. II (SS 230)

INTERMEDIATE

Recognize examples of how reformers tried to improve conditions in the cities in the 19th century.   II (SS 250)

Explain how each of the following reformers exposed urban problems: Jacob Riis, Lincoln Steffens, Thomas Nast, Upton Sinclair.   II (LA 415)

Use a generalization related to urbanization to explain factual information about urban problems in the last half of the 19th century.   III (SS 250)

SS 240   Show that you can discuss the reasons that Europeans and, later, people from other parts of the world settled in Latin America and the problems they encountered.   III (SS 320)

Recognize when and why peoples from other continents came to Latin America and how they have blended since then.   II (SS 280)

From statements taken from Latin American history, identify examples of conquest, colonization, and assimilation.   I (SS 280)

From a list, identify steps being taken by the Brazilian government to populate the interior regions of Brazil.   I (SS 375)

HISTOrY anD anTHrOPOLOGY

SS 245   Show your understanding of the changing character of rural life.   II

Describe changes taking place in farming at this time.   II

Using line graphs, charts, or written statements, explain the impact of mechanization on agriculture during the past 150 years.   II (LA 330)

Describe the advantages of city living as opposed to life in a rural area.   II (SS 225)

SOCIAL STUDIES

INTERMEDIATE

Recognize reasons that people leave a farm and go to a city to live. II (SS 225)

Recognize why people might leave the city to go live in the country. II

SS 250 **Show that you can discuss the changes that technology has made in human society and can predict changes that technology may bring about in the near future. III**

Identify correct definitions of technology, human society, and technology in human society. I

Identify the natural resources (other than air, food, and water) that people require in each of the following: primitive hunting society, agricultural society, and industrial society. I (SC 210)

Recognize two examples of artifacts. II

Find examples or pictures of artifacts related to at least ten different areas of your life as a young person in the 20th century. II

From a list of technological artifacts used by the society in which you live, recognize artifacts that represent the lowest levels of technological development and those that represent the highest levels. II

From a list of needs and wants of a colonial child and of a 20th-century child, explain how time and technology have affected the ways in which the needs and wants are met. II (SS 255)

Classify the major inventions or discoveries that transformed man from hunter-gatherer to village dweller. Explain the main effects on mankind of each invention or discovery. II (LA 345)

Write a report about an inventor whom you have interviewed or read about. Describe his experiences and explain his invention and its use. III

INTERMEDIATE

From given lists of inventions and developments of civilization, explain how the inventions caused one or more of the developments of civilization. II

Explain how the rate of change of human culture in prehistoric times compares with the rate of change in historic times. II

Collect information that indicates the causes and effects of the recent rapid interaction of cultures, especially the spread of Western technology. Classify each cause as having a positive effect or a negative effect. III

Given a list of man's inventions and activities that affect his environment, describe for each invention and activity the benefits and harms that have resulted from it. II (SS 265)

Describe suggested actions that might help solve a problem concerning natural resources. II (SS 265, SC 260)

Describe at least two advantages and at least one disadvantage of each of the following types of transportation: sailing vessels, steam-powered ships, railroads, propeller-driven airplanes, jet airplanes, gasoline-powered trucks and buses, diesel-powered trucks and buses, and animal-powered carts. II

Identify a question concerning the technology of communication or transportation in the United States that interests you. I

Describe a problem concerning the technology of communication or transportation in the United States that interests you. Suggest possible solutions. II

Discuss proposals that might help solve a problem concerning the technology of communication or transportation. III (SS 370)

Find and discuss technological information concerning communication or transportation in the United States. III (SS 370)

Using your own judgment and information you have found, suggest answers to a question concerning the technology of communication or transportation in the United States. Explain the reasons for your answers. Suggest other questions you think still need answering. II

Recognize pictures and statements supporting the idea that modern communication and transportation are "shrinking" the world (making the world seem smaller). II

Explain how the invention of the telephone, the telegraph, and the typewriter have improved communication patterns among people. II

Describe ways that the bridge, the trolley, and the subway have improved transportation in the cities. II (SS 235)

Discuss the urban problem reduced by technological developments like the following: hydrants, concrete buildings, telephones, subways, water filters, automatic sprinklers, sewage disposals, incinerators, burglar-alarm systems. III (SS 235)

Summarize ways that industrialization and urbanization have contributed to the independence and equality of the American woman. II (SS 256)

Explain why advanced technology and automation may actually make it more difficult for many minority-group members to meet their needs and wants. II

Given a description of social problems and a list of technological innovations, predict the technological innovation that is most likely to improve the social conditions described. III

Analyze a machine as if it were made of human body parts; then match the items in a list of machine parts with the most similar items in a list of human body parts. IV (SC 200)

SS 255 By forming generalizations, demonstrate your ability to perceive changing attitudes toward education and leisure time and the resultant problems in communities. IV

Describe some differences among contemporary primitive, peasant, and modern societies in attitudes towards education and leisure time. II (SS 245)

Given an activity that was considered work in colonial times and is often considered recreation today, describe reasons for this change in attitude. II (SS 205)

INTERMEDIATE

Given a list of facts, ideas, and skills, identify the ones that are usually learned formally and those usually learned informally in today's society. I

Given three reasons why the cultivation of good leisure-time activities is important for people, write a paragraph explaining each reason. III (LA 260)

Suggest at least five leisure-time activities that could be started during adolescent years and developed throughout a lifetime. Write a paragraph describing each activity. III (LA 260)

Given information about a person, such as age, size, sex, physical and mental abilities, and interests, suggest at least three leisure-time activities for that person. II (SC 210)

Conduct a survey in your community to find out what leisure-time activities are supported by community funds. III

Evaluate community-supported leisure-time activities on the basis of how well they meet the interests and needs of people of all ages, interests, economic levels, and ethnic groups. VI (SS 285)

Develop a plan for a system of community-supported leisure-time activities that would meet the interests and needs of people of all ages, interests, economic levels, and ethnic groups. V (SS 285)

SS 256 **Show that you can reasonably predict the growth and changes of the American family in relation to traditional attitudes toward family functions, social values, and other social institutions. III (SS 400, SS 420)**

Identify major changes in the American family since colonial times. Use the following criteria: (1) the role of the mother, (2) the size of the family, (3) the role of the father, (4) discipline within the family, (5) mobility of the family. I (SS 405)

Explain the term *family unit,* using examples. II

Using your own family as one example, describe the main functions of the family today. II (SS 400)

Explain the words *permissive* and *authoritarian* as they relate to the family and suggest at least three ways that authoritarianism might conflict with permissiveness in the experiences of an adolescent.   II (SS 405)

Using library resources, list functions of colonial American families and those of contemporary American families.   III (LA 325)

SS 260   Make a judgment about progress the United States has made in solving the problems of ethnic groups.   VI (SS 310)

Using two examples, explain how parts of the United States differ in culture or social groups.   II (SS 200)

Explain when and why various ethnic groups settled in the city or area where you live.   II (SS 200)

Define *slavery*. Identify reasons why slavery in America was usually confined to the black man rather than to the white man or to the Indian.   I

Describe effects of slavery on the black man.   II

Describe ways in which the blacks reacted to slavery.   II

In a one-page report or in a two-minute talk describe what is meant by the Reconstruction Period and the status of the blacks in Southern society during that time.   II

Identify five ways that blacks, despite their freed status, were discriminated against after Reconstruction.   I

Evaluate conditions of the lives of blacks living in the South, in the North, and in the West between 1880 and 1920. Tell in which of these areas in that time period you, as a black, would rather have lived and why. Include your reasons for not choosing either of the other two areas.   VI (SS 430)

Find and use information in a written report, oral report, or role-playing situation to demonstrate at least four methods that blacks have used to gain their rights in the United States.   III (SS 430)

INTERMEDIATE

By presenting the main arguments for each position in oral or written form, first support and then refute the idea that the Negro has made great progress in gaining recognition of his civil rights. III (SS 425)

Given a list of statements, determine statements that might have been made by a speaker for the integration movement and those that might have been made by a speaker for the Black Power movement. IV (SS 425)

On a map of the United States, recognize where (1) Southeast Indians and (2) Southwest Indians lived before the coming of the white man and list five major tribes within each area. For any tribe no longer occupying that area, describe the sequence of events that made them leave. II (SS 435)

Discuss the Hopi and Cherokee tribes before the coming of the white man with respect to any three of the following: housing, dress, marriage, means of food-getting, major crafts, attitude toward war. Relate each of the aspects to the tribes, natural environments and systems for survival. III

Describe the customs adapted from other tribes by the Navahos, explaining the changes made to suit the purposes of the Navahos. II

Identify three examples from American history of physical persecution of Indians by whites. I

Develop a plan to assimilate American Indians into middle-class society on a basis of equal opportunity. V (SS 285)

Explain how the life of an Indian on a reservation differs from the life of an Indian in a city or town, and tell how both differ from the representations of Indians in movies, on TV, or in stories. II

Develop a policy you think the United States government should follow with respect to Indian reservations. Explain your reasons. V (SS 260)

Write a research paper on the problems of Indians in their culture today, including information on these items: (1) policy of the federal government toward Indians today; (2) contributions of Indians to American culture; (3) differences between Indian cultures and middle-class American cultures; and (4) solutions offered by Indians and by middle-class American and government sources. Use information from all media, library sources, and interviews if possible.   III (SS 430)

Given a list of statements, identify statements that explain why the Chinese immigrant did not quickly adopt the ways of the American West.   I (SS 200)

Identify similarities and differences in United States government policy toward Chinese laborers in the 19th century and toward Mexican-American laborers in the 20th century.   I (SS 375)

List the main areas of disagreement in the strike by farm laborers against grape growers in California. Predict what changes in working conditions may come about as a result of solving the areas of disagreement.   III (SS 375).

List at least three problems common to European immigrants to the United States in the last half of the 19th century.   I (SS 200)

On a map of the world, (1) identify areas from which each of the following peoples migrated, (2) locate areas in which they settled, and (3) give dates of their migrations: Africans, Cubans, Eastern Europeans, English, Eskimos, French, Germans, Indians, Irish, Italians, Mexicans, Orientals, Puerto Ricans, Scandinavians, and Spanish.   I (SS 355)

Identify a reason why immigrants from Europe were able to escape discrimination within two or three generations whereas discrimination against blacks, Indians, Latin Americans, and Orientals has lasted much longer.   I (SS 260)

Define the following words as they are used in regard to minorities: persecution, bigotry, intolerance, and prejudice.   I (SS 425)

Given an example describing a case of group prejudice, explain why you think the people acted in such a manner.   II (LA 465)

Explain why people use stereotypes.   II (SS 400)

Recognize two or more reasons why poverty is common among some minority groups.   II (SS 260)

INTERMEDIATE

After defining a problem of a minority group of your choice, evaluate possible solutions to the problem.   VI (SS 285)

From a given list of conditions, identify conditions in Puerto Rico or New York that have contributed to the constant migration of many Puerto Rican families to New York.   I

Write a response to the following question: Have American cities helped to unite (integrate) nonwhite and white Americans as they helped unite the immigrant groups earlier in our history?   III (LA 260)

Write a paragraph describing three actions that the United States government has taken to combat prejudice in America. Give examples of the incidents you have observed and/or heard about that indicate the effectiveness or ineffectiveness of the actions.   III (SS 300)

Develop a plan to overcome or reduce the prejudices of a group of people.   V (SS 285)

Show that you can discuss the relationship between ecological problems of the world and the current focus on population control. III (SC 260)

Explain in one page or less what is meant by the "problem of overpopulation." Include such topics as future population growth, desire for better living conditions, and the supply of food and other natural resources.   II (SC 260)

Identify the three main causes of death in the world before the 19th century and explain what has been done to overcome these causes.   II (SS 235)

Given information on a country's population, number of births, and number of deaths, calculate that country's growth rate and the time that would be needed for the population to double.   II (SC 260)

Analyze this statement: "Increasing the world's food supply will not solve the problem of starvation caused by overpopulation." IV (SS 425)

Explain this statement: "Moving people from crowded areas of the world to undercrowded areas is not a satisfactory solution for the world's overpopulation problem." II (SC 260)

In one page or less, explain the mission of the planned parenthood organizations. Include at least two reasons why some people are opposed to such groups and at least two reasons why other people are in favor of them. II (SC 260)

Develop three possible plans for solving the world's overpopulation problem. Evaluate each of your plans in terms of cost, time effectiveness, and humaneness. Decide which plan would be best in view of all the criteria and explain the reason for your choice. VI (SC 260, SS 285)

Given a satisfactory solution to overpopulation agreed upon by the governments of the world, predict how the United States could help other nations to implement that solution. III (SC 260)

Given a list of various aspects of a civilization such as recreation, employment, education, housing, traffic, and pollution, explain how overpopulation can affect each. II

SS 270 Show that you can support or refute government control of drugs, alcohol, and tobacco. III (SC 225)

From a given description of symptoms, recognize symptoms that describe the physiological effects of specific drugs on the human body. II

Identify proper and improper uses of the following types of drugs: (1) amphetamines and (2) depressants. I

Identify at least one possible immediate physiological effect and one possible aftereffect on people who use marijuana. I

Identify two ways in which the improper use of drugs might be avoided. I

Write a research paper on drug abuse in which you relate drug usage to another form of deviant behavior, such as stealing. III (LA 345)

INTERMEDIATE

On the basis of a survey you have made of your peers and information you have received from mass media, write a paper discussing why people take drugs.   III

Develop a plan to influence students away from drugs in your school.   V (SS 285)

From a given description of symptoms, recognize symptoms that describe the physiological effects of alcohol on the human body.   II

Identify the path alcohol takes as it is absorbed into the blood stream and identify three principal parts of the body that are adversely affected.   I

Identify at least three reasons that people who drink alcoholic beverages give to justify their actions.   I

Identify three steps that a moderate drinker can take to prevent himself from becoming an alcoholic.   I

Identify at least three physical effects that result from cigarette smoking.   I

Given information on the relationship between smoking and disease, represent it on a bar graph.   II

Given a cigarette advertisement, determine three ways the advertisement attempts to convince people to smoke.   IV (LA 470)

SS 275   Show that you can find a variety of evidence that demonstrates the important traditions and cultural contributions made by Latin Americans and Indians to Western civilization.   III

Describe the life of the ordinary citizen in a Peruvian mountain village of today and explain how his life compares with the life of an Inca before the Spanish conquest.   II

Recognize examples of primitive, peasant, and modern ways of life within Peru.   II

List the significant contributions that each of the following Indian cultures has made to mankind: Mayan, Toltec, Aztec.   I

Write a brief report describing one of the early Indian cultures of Mexico and its importance to Mexican culture today. Include in your report the history, the type of government, the religion, and the distinctive art of the culture.   III (LA 345)

List several distinctive features of the culture of Mexico, such as customs, values, ways of adapting to the environment, social groups, and social problems.   I

Identify contributions of Indians to United States culture.   I

Write a paragraph defending this statement: "Latin Americans have made important cultural contributions to civilized life."   III

SS 280   Show your understanding of reasons for cultural and economic problems existing in Latin America today by drawing conclusions from historical and sociological data.   II

Briefly describe poor people, rich people, and middle-class people in the culture of Brazil. Recognize ways in which these classes depend on each other.   II (SS 375)

Relate the class structure of Brazil to that of the United States.   II

With at least two other classmates, discuss attitudes that the people of various racial or national groups in Brazil have toward people of other racial or national backgrounds.   III (SS 375)

Briefly describe the life styles of poor people, rich people, and middle-class people in Mexican culture.   II

Describe the opportunities for social and economic advancement available to poor people, rich people, and middle-class people in Mexican culture.   II (SS 380)

Explain how Indians, working-class people, and wealthy, powerful groups in Mexico depend on each other.   II (SS 400)

Recognize ways in which the Catholic Church has been a powerful force in the lives of the people in Latin America since the Spanish/Portuguese conquests.   II

INTERMEDIATE

From a given list of statements recognize statements that explain why in some Latin American countries there are many people who are unable to escape from a life of poverty. II (SS 375)

From a given list of social and economic problems identify the problems that are most important in Latin America today. I (SS 375)

Write a paragraph comparing the conditions of poverty in many Latin American countries with the conditions of poverty in the United States. In your paragraph consider such things as the degree of poverty and the kinds of things the governments do or do not do to help the poor people of their country. III (SS 310)

Identify from a given list of statements those that are reasons why Latin American countries have had so many violent revolutions. I (SS 305)

List at least four problems that the farmers of Latin America must face. I (SS 245)

Recognize one major agricultural problem in Latin America. II (SS 245)

Describe the differences between subsistence farming and commercial farming in Latin America. Include the following in your comparison: (1) ownership of the farms, (2) location of the farms, (3) crops that are commonly grown, (4) standard of living. II (SS 250)

Given a major agricultural problem in Latin America, develop a one-page written plan that you consider a workable solution to that problem. V (SS 285)

Develop a plan to improve the farming methods and education in the Andean countries of South America. V (SS 285)

Recognize three or four major exports of Latin America. Explain why it is dangerous for a country to depend on a single product. II (SS 375)

With at least two other classmates, predict what you think the future holds for Brazil. Support your ideas with facts that you have learned about Brazil. III (LA 230)

Describe one of Mexico's serious problems and tell what is being done to solve it. Suggest an alternate solution for the problem. II (SS 285)

Use examples of agriculture, industry, art, government, and class structure to support or reject the following statement: "Mexico is in a state of transition." III

SS 285   Demonstrate your ability to combine concepts, principles, and generalizations by developing a plan that you would support for solving a social problem.   V (SS 430)

Given a clear and simple article or statement about a social problem, recognize from a list the most accurate description of the problem. II (SS 425)

Given an article or a statement containing information about a problem, summarize the problem simply. II (LA 335)

List possible ways of directly observing a given social problem. I

From your own observations, describe the activities of people involved with solving social problems. II

Discuss a social problem of interest to you with an informed member of your community. III (LA 350)

Discuss with at least two of your classmates the opinions that each of you holds on a social issue that is subject to differing viewpoints. III (LA 230, SS 425)

After defining a problem involving education or group relations in your school, develop a plan for solving the problem. V (SS 400)

Develop a plan for cutting the school year to six months. V (SS 255)

Develop a plan that would satisfy a social goal. Your plan should be (1) relevant, (2) stated in the simplest terms possible, and (3) easy to follow. V

INTERMEDIATE

Compare different proposals for solving a problem concerning human relations and decide which you would endorse. VI (SS 425)

Develop a plan to solve a social problem and interview a public official concerning your plan. V (LA 230)

Predict causes for the difficulties encountered in the implementation of a plan adopted for solving a social problem.

Support your position on a social issue involving differing viewpoints. Present your viewpoint to a group. III (LA 225)

Evaluate the validity of your stand on a social issue involving differing viewpoints. VI

Evaluate a plan of action you have developed for some human resource problem. VI

Identify an unjust social situation that needs attention, and write a petition to an appropriate person or agency in a position to either correct the situation or influence a change in the situation. The petition should (1) be directed to a person or agency that can help, (2) identify a law that needs correction or a situation that needs attention, and (3) include reasonable suggestions for correcting the situation. III (SS 430)

Given a description of a social problem and a list of possible solutions, recognize the solution that would be most acceptable to the people involved. II (SS 400)

Given a description of a social problem and differing viewpoints on the problem, suggest reasons for these viewpoints. II

Given a social issue involving differing viewpoints, discuss your viewpoint with a group. III

Given a goal requiring group cooperation, develop a plan for achieving the goal and present it to a group. V (SS 400)

Using specific guidelines, lead a group in discussing a social problem and arriving at a possible solution to the problem. The guidelines are (1) to have all members of the group participate and express an opinion concerning the problem; (2) to express no specific opinion yourself; (3) to encourage participants to support their views.   III (LA 235)

Develop a community study project, using primary sources to compile your data. Present a written report of your findings in which you recommend possible reforms or improvements.   V

To show how members of your community might cooperate with one another, lead or participate in a panel discussion in which serious community problems are listed and possible solutions to these problems are discussed.   III

Develop a plan of action for dealing with a problem concerning human relations in the United States. Outline the steps you would follow in carrying out the plan.   V (SS 400)

In a discussion or a written paragraph, cite different values or customs in American society. Suggest ways in which individuals with these different values or customs can solve problems cooperatively without conflict.   III (SS 255)

POLITICAL SCIENCE

SS 290   Show your understanding of the effect on the writers of the American Constitution of attempts to organize a government structure in colonial America.   II (SS 205)

Identify characteristics of the structure of the government and the major powers granted Congress under the Articles of Confederation.   I

Describe critical weaknesses of the Articles of Confederation and tell about problems that resulted because of the nature of the government under the Confederation. Be able to describe at least one problem in each of the following areas: land expansion, finance, foreign relations.   II (SS 205)

INTERMEDIATE

Identify qualifications or contributions of the following men at the Constitutional Convention: George Washington, Robert Morris, Alexander Hamilton, Benjamin Franklin, James Madison. I

Describe the following plans and compromises made at the Constitutional Convention: the Virginia Plan, the New Jersey Plan, the Connecticut Compromise, the Three-fifths Compromise, the Commerce and Slave Trade Compromise. The description should include what the concern or problem was and the solutions proposed. II

Describe the major questions that arose out of the struggle for Constitutional ratification on the following issues: states' rights vs. federal power, guarantees for individual rights. Include specific issues, leaders, viewpoints, and compromises. II

Referring to the United States Constitution, recognize specific sections pertaining to the following principles of government: sovereignty of the people or voters, supreme law of the land, division of powers between national and state governments, equality of states, doctrine of limited powers, doctrine of separation of powers—checks and balances, guaranteed rights, provisions for growth. II

Match the structural provisions as established in the Constitution with the appropriate branches of government: legislative, executive, judicial. (Structural provisions include terms of office, elections, powers and duties, etc.) I

SS 295   By analyzing statements on current issues, demonstrate your ability to perceive conflicts among United States political leaders over the purpose and role of government. List current conflicts and conflicts among early American political leaders. IV (SS 425)

Identify examples of how Jefferson's Republican party accepted or compromised with some of the programs and philosophies of the Federalist. I

Describe important economic, social, and political transitions that came about between the times of Jefferson and Jackson. Cite possible American values that might account for these changes. II

INTERMEDIATE

Given a short summary or description of an event concerning governmental policy, federal legislation, or a decision of the Supreme Court in the first half of the 1800's, conclude whether this event reflects a feeling of nationalism or a tendency toward sectionalism. Be able to justify your conclusion. II (LA 225)

Recognize controversial topics, opinions, generalizations, and/or arguments presented on a TV panel program such as "Meet the Press" or "Face the Nation." II (LA 465)

Using as examples some successful and some unsuccessful attempts by the government to compromise, explain the importance of compromise in stabilizing a democratic government. II (SS 210)

SS 300 Demonstrate your ability to perceive the relationship of civilian control problems to civil rights. IV (SS 270, SS 310, SS 330)

Given the following list of events, put them in chronological order and briefly describe each. II
1. Founding of the N.A.A.C.P.
2. *Plessy* v. *Ferguson*
3. *Brown* v. *Board of Education*
4. March on Washington (led by Martin Luther King)
5. Montgomery bus boycott
6. Newark and Watts riots

Recognize instances in which individuals with unpopular views or appearance have been improperly and illegally denied their civil liberties by government authorities and/or other citizens. II (SS 330)

Given a list of arguments on censorship, recognize those which defend censorship and those which are opposed to censorship. II (SS 330)

SS 305 Demonstrate your ability to perceive relationships between political problems and legislative action. IV

Match the following political terms with their definitions: campaign, party, election, ballot, convention, nominate, primary election, plurality. I

INTERMEDIATE

Develop a list of criteria that a local legislator might follow to arrive at a stand or a decision on a local problem.   V

Suggest ways in which a special interest group might influence a governmental decision.   II

Given material related to a current political problem, recognize the major issues that must be considered in the solution of that problem.   II (SS 285)

After interviewing a businessman, a student, and a social worker on a controversial issue, summarize the position of each on the issue.   III (SS 425)

SS 310   Show that you can discuss basic needs that should be met by the laws and rules of a society.   III

Discuss cases where speech is clearly protected by the Constitution as interpreted by the Supreme Court and cases where it is not. List the advantages to the individual citizen and to society of protecting freedom of speech.   III (SS 315)

Discuss cases where assembly is clearly protected by the Constitution as interpreted by the Supreme Court and cases where it is not. List the advantages to the individual citizen and to society of protecting freedom of assembly.   III (SS 315)

Support your own views on freedom of religion and when and if it should be limited. Include views on the separation of church and state. Recognize advantages of having freedom of religion protected by the Constitution.   III (SS 420)

List examples of how state, city, or town governments perform each of the following: (1) provide ordinary services to people, and (2) protect individuals and keep order.   I

Explain the organization of city and county governments and describe some of the services provided by each to the urban community.   II

Summarize information about local government services to individuals. Write the summary as an argument for support of local government.   II (LA 335)

Classify local governmental services received from two sources according to type of service. Explain how the services could be combined or separated.   II

Given a list of rights and responsibilities of a citizen, differentiate them.   II

Identify some of the rights we enjoy as American citizens. Identify some duties and responsibilities citizens have to their country.   I (SS 330)

Suggest ways in which Americans display good citizenship.   II (SS 330)

Suggest common causes for rules and laws.   II

Suggest events that led to the writing of given rules and laws.   II

Develop a strategy or plan that could be followed by a small group of people (5–100) in order to formulate rules and make decisions.   V (SS 285, SS 400)

Classify the characteristics of a plan for small-group formulation of rules and decision-making as democratic, oligarchic, or dictatorial.   II (SS 325)

SS 315   Demonstrate your ability to combine concepts, principles, and generalizations by developing a set of political values based on information you have analyzed.   V

Explain the meaning of *citizen, right,* and *duty.*   II

Write a paragraph supporting or rejecting the following statement: "Our form of government gives us many political freedoms, but these freedoms are not absolute because there are exceptions to each of them."   III (SS 295, LA 345)

Discuss characteristics of men willing to serve their country by fighting in battle.   III (SS 420)

Recognize several sacrifices that must be made by a person serving in public office.   II (SS 420)

INTERMEDIATE

After listening to a political or editorial speech of at least 5 minutes on TV, radio, a record, or tape, describe in two or three sentences (1) the main idea of the speech, and (2) two or three subordinate ideas that contribute to the main idea.   II (LA 465)

Given a written copy of a person-to-person interview you have just listened to on tape, recognize comments spoken by the interviewed person that are irrelevant to the main topic.   II (SS 425)

Recognize the following signs of bias in a taped radio newscast: loaded words, exaggeration, and statements of opinion or prediction presented as fact.   II (SS 425)

SS 320   Show that you can find and use information from both sides of the issue to write a summary of the advantages and disadvantages of two or more solutions that have been offered for a current conflict between nations.   III (SS 425)

Using one sentence for each, describe three current conflicts in the Western Hemisphere.   II

List major world problems. Your list should include at least five general problems.   I

Explain briefly the historical significance of the following: (1) French Indo-China War, (2) Dien Bien Phu, (3) Geneva Convention, (4) Viet Cong, (5) National Liberation Front, (6) Nguyen Cao Ky, (7) Ho Chi Minh, (8) the Ho Chi Minh Trail.   II

Identify at least five nonmilitary goals that the United States is trying to achieve in South Vietnam.   I

Discuss how the United States is and is not fulfilling this definition of greatness in fighting a war in Vietnam: "Greatness lies not in being strong, but in the proper use of strength."   III (SS 315)

Using (1) news reports, (2) news analyses, (3) position papers, and (4) interviews with acquaintances, write a paragraph discussing effects of the goals and events of the Vietnam conflict on other aspects of American life.   III (LA 345)

Given a description of a conflict between nations, differentiate between causes and effects of the conflict. II

Given an unsolved world problem, describe its possible international implications. II

SS 325 Show that you can discuss the political features of a country. III

Define the following terms and identify at least one example in Latin America for each term: colony, republic, dictatorship, democracy. I

From statements taken from Latin American history, identify examples of conquest, colonization, and assimilation. I

Given a list of statements, classify them as examples of autocracy or as examples of democracy. II

With three or more classmates, write and act an original script on "Democracy and Dictatorship in Action." III (LA 440)

Given reference materials, describe the United States, Great Britain, Saudi Arabia, and Cuba in terms of the following political characteristics: (1) the method used to choose leaders, (2) the title given to the main leader or leaders, (3) the length of time the main leader or leaders are in office, (4) the method used to remove the leader from office. II (SS 315)

SS 330 Show your understanding of the relationship of problems of individuals to their form of government. II (SS 300)

From a given list of problems identify the problems that most Latin American countries must solve in order to have governments that truly represent the people. I

From a given list of statements identify statements that explain why Latin American countries have had so many violent revolutions. I (SS 280)

After reading short stories about people seeking freedom, explain whether they were seeking religious, political, academic, or economic freedom. II (LA 395)

GeOGraPHY

SS 335 Show that you can use maps and globes to find information. III (SS 435)

Explain orally how to proceed from your present position or a place that you select to one other place in the school, on the playground, and in the neighborhood. Reverse the process.   II (LA 225)

Explain the purpose of a map legend.   II

Given symbols on a road map, identify their meanings by using the map legend. Include population density of cities, map scale, and transportation symbols and routes.   I

On a given map, locate the intermediate directions northeast, southeast, northwest, and southwest.   I

Locate points on a map by using the map's coordinates.   I

Tell one practical use for each of the following types of maps: topographical, road, population, and weather.   I

Using a map of the United States and the eight major directions of the compass (N, NE, E, SE, S, SW, W, and NW), describe how to travel from the place where you live to five other cities marked on the map.   II

Using a street map of your city or local area, explain how to proceed from your house or school to a point of interest in your community. Include street names, directions, and distances (two blocks, etc.).   II

On an outline map or globe, label from memory each continent with its correct name.   I

Using a map with a scale, measure the distance between places marked on the map.   II

After measuring an area or object, use a simple scale to make a drawing of it.   III

Given a time of day in your zone and a map showing time-zone boundaries, tell the time of day in any other zone in the United States. II

Identify the conditions that cause the earth to have night and day. I (SC 365)

Explain how time zones are set up so that clocks relate to sun time around the world. II

Using a globe, locate the great-circle route. Give the distance in miles between any two locations. II

Using a globe, locate any position when its latitude and longitude are given. II

Using a globe and given the time of day for one location, find the time of day for any location on earth. II

Using a globe, locate specific places at a given latitude. II

Using a globe, locate specific places at a given longitude. II

Given a topographic map showing the following features, locate each feature using the map legend. II

Natural features	Man-made features
Bay	Airplane route
Delta	Airport
Desert	Bridge
Falls	Church
Island	Dam
Isthmus	Railroad
Lake	Road
Peninsula	School
River	Ship Channel
Strait	Swamp

Using only direction, road numbers, and numbers of miles, write instructions for driving between any two given points on a road map. III

On a political map or globe locate the United States (including Alaska and Hawaii), Canada, and Mexico. I

INTERMEDIATE

Given any list of countries on a political map, classify and locate Central America, the West Indies, and South America. II

On a political map or globe locate the countries of Eastern and Western Europe. I

Locate the following countries on a political map of the Middle East: Turkey, Lebanon, Israel, Jordan, Egypt, Saudi Arabia, Iraq, Iran, and Syria. I

Locate the following countries on a political map or globe: Union of South Africa, Ethopia, Kenya, Northern Rhodesia, Nigeria, the Congo, Libya, Algeria, and Morocco. I

Locate the following countries on a political map of Asia: Russia, Red China, Nationalist China, Japan, North Korea, South Korea, North Vietnam, South Vietnam, Laos, Cambodia, Thailand, Burma, the Philippines, India, and Tibet. I

SS 340 Show your understanding of weather conditions and methods of predicting, measuring, and recording weather conditions. II (SC 365)

Tell the difference between weather and climate. Tell what atmospheric conditions are characteristic of each. I

Identify the basic cloud types (cumulus, cirrus, and stratus) when given drawings or descriptions of these cloud formations. I

Match the different forms of precipitation (rain, sleet, hail, snow) with descriptions of how each precipitation is formed. I

Recognize the four kinds of weather fronts (warm, cold, stationary, and occluded) when given descriptions or examples of each weather front. II

Recognize definitions of destructive forces of weather (thunderstorm, cyclone, typhoon, hurricane, and tornado) when given descriptions or diagrams of each storm. II

Using world maps, or globes showing ocean currents and air pressure areas, recognize clockwise and counterclockwise ocean currents. Describe how wind is related to high and low pressure areas. II

Keep a daily record of your observations of elements of weather for two weeks. Use reports from the weather bureau for recording any information you cannot personally observe.   III

Given information about factors that cause movement of air masses (angle of sun's rays, night and day temperatures and other factors that cause unequal heating), predict the probable direction of air movement.   III

Given a description of a weather condition, name the correct instrument for measuring and recording the condition.   I

Match the tools used by meteorologists (electronic computers, radar, radiosonde, weather balloons and satellites) with their functions in predicting weather.   I

Given a weather map with a legend, describe the weather conditions of specific areas on the map.   II

Given readings from recording instruments (thermometer, barometer, and hygrometer), predict changes in the weather.   III

SS 345   Show your understanding of climate conditions and their causes.   II

Identify typical characteristics of the following five basic climates: tropical, dry, mild-winter moist, cold-winter moist, and polar.   I

Using reference sources including an outline map of the world, identify and label locations of the five basic earth climates: tropical, dry, mild-winter moist, cold-winter moist, and polar.   I (SS 355)

Using a detailed map of an area, describe the location of the area in relation to the prime meridian and equator. Describe the climate as either tropical, dry, mild-winter moist, cold-winter moist, or polar.   II

Using reference sources, including a map of Latin America, locate three examples showing how latitude affects the climate of a region.   III (SS 355)

INTERMEDIATE

Using reference sources, including a map of Latin America, locate three examples showing how altitude affects the climate of a region.   III (SS 355)

Locate and describe the hot-weather zone, or tropics, of Latin America.   II

Given one geographic region of the world, use reference sources, including maps, to describe how the following conditions affect the region's climate: latitude, elevation, oceans (large bodies of water), landforms, and winds.   III

Given a climate map and an outline map of the same area, interpret the climate map by relating the climate to the outline map.   II

Given the rainfall and temperature of each month of the year for any city, represent on a graph the relationship between rainfall and temperature.   III

Recognize the positions of a given point on earth in relation to the sun during fall, winter, spring, and summer. Explain how temperature changes at this point are because of these changes in position.   II

Describe the effects that elevation, latitude, and nearness to water have on temperature.   II

SS 350 Show your understanding of the influence of physical environment on people's lives.   II

Using two examples, explain how life styles in the United States depend partly on natural environment.   II

Explain why the plateau regions of the low latitudes near the equator are heavily populated, while the plateaus of the middle latitudes are sparsely populated.   II (SS 345)

Explain how climate is a factor in deciding what kind of home to build in the following regions: polar, tropical rain forest, and desert.   II

INTERMEDIATE

Explain what is meant by adapting to environment both biologically and culturally. Cite two examples of races adapting to their environments. II (SC 230)

Given the climatic conditions of an area, use your atlas to determine which of the following crops could be grown in that area: wheat, sugar beets, rice, or cotton. III (SC 230)

On an unmarked map of South America, locate the following: (1) Andes Mountains, (2) Amazon basin, (3) major grasslands, (4) tropical climates, and (5) temperate climates. I (SS 355)

Tell ways in which the Andes Mountains influence (1) the climates in Peru, (2) the people there. I

Briefly describe the effects of elevation on climatic regions and general culture (way of life) in Mexico. II

Infer how Latin American customs and ways of adapting to the environment serve local human needs. II

SS 355 **Show that you can use resource maps, globes, atlases, and related reference books to collect information about natural resources and human activities, including agriculture and production. III**

Identify the geographic time and location of early civilizations including Egypt, Mesopotamia, ancient India and China, Greece, Rome, Byzantium, ancient African kingdoms, pre-Columbian civilizations in America, Medieval and Renaissance Europe. I

On a map of the world, identify where and when the following peoples migrated to North America. I

1. Africans	6. French	11. Mexicans
2. Cubans	7. Germans	12. Orientals
3. East Europeans	8. Indians	13. Puerto Ricans
4. English	9. Irish	14. Scandinavians
5. Eskimos	10. Italians	15. Spanish

Identify the most densely populated parts of the United States. I

SOCIAL STUDIES

INTERMEDIATE

Using a map that shows the density of population in the United States, classify three settled locations as urban, three as suburban, and three as rural. II

Classify names of materials and products imported into the United States as raw materials, agricultural products, or manufactured products. II

Represent with a graph the kinds of mineral fuels used to heat homes of students in your class. II

On a map showing natural resources, agricultural products, transportation routes, and physical features of an imaginary country, demonstrate the relation between these factors and the best location for each of the following types of cities: (1) port, (2) steel manufacturing, and (3) food processing. III

Use the necessary reference materials to arrange the following nations in order of ability to produce raw materials needed for food and for each of their major industries: United States, Canada, France, Germany, India, Japan, United Kingdom, and U.S.S.R. III

On a population distribution map of the world, locate and name the two continents that have the largest concentration of human resources. I

Using any reference books, identify the country that produces the largest quantity of each of the following crops: cotton, corn, rice, and wheat. III (LA 330)

Describe a situation in which a country either lacks or has misused one of the following resources: grass, soil, minerals, trees, or water. II (SC 260)

Given a map showing world mineral production, use your atlas to determine whether the map is showing the locations of bauxite, coal, copper, iron, lead, oil (petroleum), tin, or zinc mines. III

For each of the following products, locate on an outline map of Latin America the country that produces the most of that product: cacao, coffee, cattle, sheep, sugar, and wheat. I

Locate the major crop-producing region on a map of Brazil. I

Recognize three or four major exports of Latin America. Explain why it is dangerous for a country to depend upon a single product. II

SS 360 Show that you can use resources and references to plan a month-long trip for your family. III (SS 435)

Use reference books, maps, and travel folders to find information about Latin American countries that interest you. Use your information to plan an itinerary for an imaginary month-long trip to Latin America for yourself and your family. Describe your reasons for visiting each place. III

From a variety of travel folders and brochures, prepare a budget for your family's transportation, food, and lodging on a month-long trip. Your total budget must not exceed $5000. III

Find information on climate and weather conditions in the places you will visit for the appropriate season. Describe the type of clothing you will need to take. III

Prepare a list of problems and/or difficult situations your family might encounter on the trip. Describe how each problem might be solved. III (SS 395)

Prepare a presentation for your class about your trip. Describe your preparations and illustrate your presentation with pictures of places you plan to visit. III

SS 365 Make a judgment on the effectiveness of an ecology program that is in progress or has been recently proposed. VI (SC 260)

Explain how each of ten natural resources is used by man. II

Classify a list of natural resources according to (1) whether they were developed early in the history of a country or settlement, or (2) whether complicated tools were required before they could be used. II (SS 205)

Identify the governmental agencies or private organizations in your community that are responsible for preventing air and water pollution. I (SS 310)

INTERMEDIATE

Tell how your community disposes of waste materials.   I

Given a map of your community, (1) identify the source of your local water supply, (2) describe the type of purification process used, and (3) trace the route and system of sewage and garbage disposal.   I (SC 210)

Identify ways that private citizens can work independently or in groups to ensure clean air and clean water.   I

Develop a plan for improving the quality of air, water, and sewage disposal in your community. Include information concerning cost, time, and effectiveness. Present this plan to the appropriate governing agency in your local community.   V (SC 260)

Explain how pollution and congestion affect individuals and deprive them of individual freedom.   II (SC 260)

Using two examples, explain how parts of the United States differ in the following ways: climate, natural resources, pollution.   II

Identify a problem that interests you concerning natural resources in the United States.   I

Find information that will help answer a question concerning natural resources in the United States. Use the information in a written or oral report.   III (LA 335)

Name causes of air pollution. Identify ways to prevent pollution of our air.   I

Name causes of water pollution. Identify ways to prevent pollution of our water.   I

Using your own judgment and information you have learned, suggest answers to a question concerning natural resources in the United States. Explain the reasons for your answers. Explain what questions you think still need answering.   II (SS 285)

Describe a problem concerning natural resources in the United States that interests you. Suggest possible solutions.   II (SS 365)

Given a list of man's inventions and activities that affect his environment, describe the benefits and harms that have resulted from each invention and activity.   II (SC 260)

Compare and contrast suggested actions that might help solve a problem concerning natural resources.   VI (SS 365)

Evaluate a plan of action that you have developed for a natural resource problem.   VI (SS 285)

Describe a current problem involving conservation of a natural resource. List suggestions by individuals who would aid in promoting the needed conservation.   II (SS 310)

Research a current ecological program and evaluate its effectiveness according to your knowledge of the social, economic, and physical problems involved.   VI (SS 425)

Given a list of various aspects of a civilization, such as recreation, employment, education, housing, traffic, and pollution, explain how overpopulation can affect each aspect.   II (SC 260)

Develop a plan for dealing with one of the problems caused by man's changing his environment. Include the following: (1) description of the problem, (2) desired outcomes, (3) information that bears on the problem, (4) causes and effects of the problem, (5) comparison of possible solutions, (6) your evaluation of the best possible solution, and (7) criteria for judging how well the plan works.   V (SS 285)

economics

SS 370   Show that you can discuss interrelationships that exist in an economy where natural resources, human resources, and means of production are not located in the same place.   III (SS 350)

List the criteria you would have to consider before establishing a manufacturing business.   I

Explain orally, in writing, or with diagrams the interrelationship that exists among (1) labor, (2) tools, (3) natural resources, and (4) material human desires.   II

INTERMEDIATE

Support the location of a given industry by using the concept of "easy access to necessary resources" as the basis of your support. III

Explain why the development of industries is a primary cause of urbanization.   II (SS 230)

On a population distribution map of the world, locate and name the two continents that have the largest concentration of human resources.   I (SS 355)

Identify a problem that interests you concerning human resources in the United States.   I

Find information concerning human resources in the United States and use it in a written report.   III

Using your own judgment and information you have learned, suggest answers to the question concerning human resources in the United States. Explain the reasons for your answers. Explain what questions you think still need answering.   II

Describe a problem that interests you concerning human resources in the United States. Suggest possible solutions.   II

Compare and contrast proposals that might help solve a problem concerning human resources.   VI (SS 285)

From a list of reasons, select reasons that correctly state why countries trade.   I

Given a list of goods and services, suggest whether the area where the goods are produced or the service is offered is likely to be urban, suburban, or rural.   II

Using two examples, explain how parts of the United States differ in ways most people earn their living.   II

Recognize three or four major exports of Latin America. Explain why it is dangerous for a country to depend on a single product. II (SS 355)

SOCIAL STUDIES

SS 375   Show that you can use economic concepts and terms in discussing current events.   III

Tell the meaning of *barter*. Tell the two conditions necessary before bartering can take place. Name items people used for barter in ancient times.   I

Identify items used for money before metal was used.   I

Describe the initial usage of coined money instead of earlier means of exchange and tell why coined money was an improvement. Explain one disadvantage of using coined money exclusively.   II

Explain why paper money as well as coined money is used today. Explain how the government of a country controls the use of paper money.   II

Given the following economic terms, match each term with its definition.   I

1. Profit	8. Consumption
2. Loss	9. Producer
3. Resources	10. Worker
4. Choices	11. Production
5. Labor	12. Distribution
6. Service	13. Laborer
7. Consumer	14. Economic

Given a list of news headlines and a list of economic statements, recognize the statement that best explains the headline.   II

Define each of the following economic terms: consumption, production, distribution, trading, pricing, profit, and capital.   I

SS 380   Show that you can discuss the features of an economy that place it in a particular economic category.   III

Given descriptions of the economies of three underdeveloped countries—India, Spain, and Saudi Arabia—recognize characteristics common to underdeveloped countries.   II

Describe differences between (1) a free-enterprise economy, (2) a mixed economy, and (3) a planned economy.   II

INTERMEDIATE

Given a description of an economic system and a list of countries, recognize the country that most closely resembles the description. II

Analyze the use of one of the following by the United States and Latin America: (1) profits and wealth, (2) human resources, (3) technology. IV

SS 385   Show that you can use mathematical skills in solving personal economic problems.   III

Given the hourly wage and number of hours worked in a week, determine weekly, monthly, and annual wages. III

Given the times in and out, the company's regular work hours, overtime, and any sick leave and annual leave taken, complete a time card for one week. I

Given the number of pieces of work completed daily for a week and the rate per piece, determine the weekly wage. III

Given a salary and the deductions, determine the amount of take-home pay. III

Given an itemized list of expenditures and the annual income for a family, determine the percent of income spent for each item. III

Given the amount of annual income and the percent of income to be spent on various items, determine the amount to be allocated to each item in a monthly budget. III

Given the cost of a specific quantity of a product and the cost of a different quantity of the same product, determine the cost per unit for both quantities to learn which rate is cheaper. III

Given a list of purchased items, the amount charged for each item, and the sales tax rate, demonstrate how a sales slip would show the price of each item, the tax, and the total bill. III

Given the total bill and the amount paid to the cashier, determine the number and variety of bills and/or coins to be given in change. III

Given the appropriate table of fares, find the cost of travel by plane, bus, ship, or train between any two cities. II

Given the average speed and gas mileage for a car, the cost of gas, and the distance between two cities, determine traveling time and cost of gas for a trip in this car between two cities. III

Given a table of parcel-post rates and information about the distance between cities, find the cost of mailing a given package from one city to any other city in the United States. II

Given a table of rates for first-class mail, air mail, special delivery, and registered mail, find the cost of mailing a given letter or package first class, air mail, special delivery, or registered. II

Given a table of rates for freight, express, and air express, find the cost of shipping a given package in one of these three ways. II

Given a schedule of rates for electricity and an electric bill from which the number of kilowatt hours used can be determined, determine the total cost of the electricity used and tell how this cost compares with the amount shown on the electric bill. III

Given a schedule of rates for gas and a gas bill from which the number of cubic feet used can be determined, determine the total cost of the gas used and tell how this cost compares with the amount shown on the gas bill. III

Given a schedule of rates for water and a water bill from which the number of cubic feet used can be determined, determine the total cost of the water used and tell how this cost compares with the amount shown on the water bill. III

Given a table of telephone rates, the type and number of calls made in a given month, and the telephone bill for the month, determine the total cost of the phone service for the month (including federal and local taxes). Tell how this amount compares with the total shown on the telephone bill. III

Given a table of annual premiums for three types of life insurance coverage (straight life, limited life, and endowment), the amount and type of insurance purchased, and the age of the policy-holder at the time of purchase, determine what percent of the total amount of the policy he will have paid in premiums in n years. III

INTERMEDIATE

Given a table of annual premiums for bodily injury, property damage, comprehensive damage, and collision insurance for different types of driving, determine the total annual premium for adequate coverage for a specific model car used for pleasure, driving to work, or business.   III

Given the annual premium rates of coverage for fire insurance and the amount of coverage, determine the premium for one year.   II

Given the original price of a car, its age, and its trade-in or resale value, determine the average annual depreciation of the car.   III

Given the original cost and average annual depreciation of a car, determine the rate of depreciation.   III

Given the annual payments for taxes, insurance, gasoline, oil, repairs, interest, and depreciation, determine the total annual operating cost and average monthly operating cost of a car.   III

Given an itemized list of college expenditures (including tuition, room and board, books, travel expenses, and personal expenses) for one month or year, determine the cost of attending college for four years.   III

Given the present average cost of attending college for one year and the predicted average rate of increase, predict the annual cost in n years.   III

Given the amount of a scholarship for one year and the total annual cost of college, determine the percent of the total that is paid by the scholarship.   III

Given the total cost for one year of college, determine how much you would have to save yearly for any given number of years (without considering interest you might earn or cost of inflation) to pay for one year of college.   III

Given the average yearly wage for an occupation and average years of employment in that occupation, determine the average total life income for a person in that occupation.   III

PSYCHOLOGY and PHILOSOPHY

SS 395 Show that you can recognize personal problems and apply problem-solving skills and human-relations skills to their solution.   III (SS 285)

Given a picture or a series of pictures illustrating human situations, suggest at least one personal problem found in each.   II

Given a list of statements about a personal problem, recognize which statement defines the problem most clearly.   II

Given a simulated personal problem situation, explain the problem clearly.   II (SS 395)

Determine the personal problems involved in a social conflict on a television program, in a movie, in real life, or in a role-playing situation.   IV

Present sensible criteria by which an ordinary personal decision could be made to solve a conflict.   III

Given a series of social situations, recognize conditions that contain personal conflict.   II

Describe a personal conflict that you have noticed in your home, classroom, or community.   II

Given a conflict and several statements on the conflict, recognize the statement that gives a solution.   II

Given a case study involving conflict, describe the conflict and suggest reasons that it exists.   II

SS 400 Show that you understand the importance of interpersonal relationships in solving social problems.   II

After defining a problem of education or group relations in your school, develop a plan for solving the problem.   V

INTERMEDIATE

Analyze data that you have collected to determine the relationship between social problems in your school and those in your community. Form committees and obtain information through interviews, questionnaires, open-discussion groups, and debates.   IV

Select a question concerning human relations in the United States that interests you.   II

Find information concerning human relations in the United States and use it in a written or oral report.   III

Suggest questions concerning human relations in the United States you think still need answering. Explain the reasons for your answers.   II

Describe a problem concerning human relations in the United States that interests you. Suggest possible solutions.   II

SS 405   Demonstrate your ability to perceive problems of teenagers by analyzing specific problems on the basis of both experience and information.   IV

Present five problems common today to adolescents in their early teens, and present a solution for one of them that will probably be acceptable to most teenagers.   III

In each of three examples showing conflict between the adolescent's need for independence and his need for dependence, explain how the two needs conflict.   II

Using examples, explain the characteristics of conformity and of self-reliance displayed by adolescents.   II

Explain what is meant by the "generation gap," and in a specific example state both the adolescent's and his two parents' viewpoints regarding one of the following: (1) curfews, (2) styles of dress, (3) forms of entertainment, (4) political beliefs.   II

Develop a program of activities that would help eliminate some of the adult-student conflicts in your community.   V

Conduct an interview with fellow students about a subject of concern to them, such as dating. Make up a question sheet and record and summarize the information gained.   III

"The first years of dating are filled with fear, unhappiness, and embarrassment and hardly seem worth the experience." Support or refute the entire statement or parts of it.   III

Given a list of laws, suggest reasons to explain which laws teenagers are the more likely to break and which ones they are less likely to break.   II

Predict the possible consequences to yourself, your family, your friends, and your country if you participate in a civil protest.   III (SS 315)

Develop a hypothesis about the causes of juvenile delinquency and present some possible ways to reduce juvenile delinquency, based upon what you have considered the causes. You may use a format like this: "I believe that poor schools are the major cause of juvenile delinquency. I base this upon . . ."   IV

Conduct an interview with at least one police officer, asking the following questions and recording the answers to them.   III (LA 350)
1. What do you consider to be a major cause of juvenile delinquency?
2. What laws do you see teenagers break most often?
3. Why did you become an officer?
4. What are the legal requirements for becoming an officer?
5. What is the most difficult job for an officer?
6. What formal training do you have to have to become an officer?

Prepare and present a report on the recreational, cultural, educational, and employment opportunities that your community provides specifically for youth. Discuss the appropriateness of existing facilities to the needs of your community.   III (SS 285)

Participate in an open-ended group discussion on teenage problems in which no one solution is apparent.   III (LA 230)
1. Define the topic.
2. Contribute relevant ideas.
3. Contribute to the resolution of the problem.
4. State whether or not you think your contribution was worthwhile.

INTERMEDIATE

SS 410   Show your understanding of aspects of careers in the following occupational areas: industrial trade, business, commercial service and health service.   II

Identify the typical work activities of machinists.   I

Identify the typical work activities of tool and die makers.   I

Identify the main tasks of the following types of printing workers: composing room, platemaking, printing press.   I

Identify various jobs that are included in the family of industrial trade occupations.   I

List three common means of learning industrial trades.   I

List the main duties of a business manager.   I

Describe the differences among the jobs of first-level, middle-level, and top-level managers.   I

Identify how much education is generally required for a business manager.   I

Identify the job opportunities for managers.   I

List the typical work activities of accountants.   I

List the typical work activities and employment opportunities for advertising workers.   I

List the typical work activities of purchasing agents.   I

List the typical activities of airline pilots.   I

Identify various jobs that are included in the family of business occupations.   I

List two common ways to prepare for the occupation of cosmetologist.   I

Identify the employment opportunities for cooks and chefs. I

List the typical work activities of waiters or waitresses. I

Identify various occupations that are included in the family of service occupations. I

Identify the educational requirements that a student must meet in order to become a physician. I

List two factors that a recent graduate of a college of dentistry would consider in setting up a dental office. I

List the typical work activities of pharmacists employed in drugstores, in hospitals, and as drug salesmen. I

List three types of institutions that offer training programs for professional nurses and tell the length of each program. I

Identify various occupations that are included in the family of health-service occupations. I

Compare the length of training required and the average salary for a licensed practical nurse and for a professional nurse. II

SS 415 **Demonstrate your ability to combine concepts, principles, and generalizations by selecting at least two major world religions (not your own) and by developing a project (report, diary, story, panorama, collage) that illustrates how religions affect daily activities. V**

Choose six of the following religions and locate on a world outline map the region of the world where each originated: Judaism, Confucianism, Buddhism, Sikhism, Hinduism, Christianity, Taoism, Islam, Zoroastranism, Shintoism, Jainism. I

Represent in a graph the five religions that most of the people in the world believe in. II

Explain the rules of behavior for five religions of the world. Draw a diagram or make a chart that demonstrates similarities or differences among the religions in the rules of behavior. III

INTERMEDIATE

Prepare and present a report about the conditions that support the development of a religion in a country.   III

Write a paragraph describing the role of religion in one country.   III

Recognize ways in which the Catholic Church has been a powerful force in the lives of the people in Latin America since the Spanish/Portuguese conquests.   II

Write a research paper on the contemporary religious trends of American society, relating concern with religion to awareness of social problems. Use your information to predict the form and direction that religion may take in the next century.   III (SS 430)

SS 420   Demonstrate your ability to combine concepts, principles, and generalizations by developing a set of social values based on information pertaining to a specific problem you have analyzed.   V

Explain how we judge one civilization to be more advanced than another. Explain why you think a so-called more advanced civilization may or may not be more satisfying to live in than a less advanced one.   II

Recognize a definition of the term *society* that applies to nonhuman societies as well as to human societies.   II

Write a report on a specific nonhuman society based on the following questions.   III
1. How is the society organized?
2. How is a leader chosen?
3. What are the food requirements?
4. What kind of shelters do they build?
5. What or who are their enemies?
6. What kind of system of rewards or punishments do they have?
7. How do they defend themselves?
8. What is the role of the individual?
9. What is the role of the family?
10. What does the society produce and how is it done?
11. What are the main problems of the society?

Describe characteristics that are desirable and those that are undesirable in friends.   II (SS 400)

Using an ordinary day in your life as a guide, suggest at least two rules for self-protection and two rules for preventing you from harming other people.   II (SS 400)

Demonstrate tolerance of others by dramatizing situations in which there are people who have ideas that are different from your own. III (LA 445)

Predict the possible consequences to yourself, your family, your friends, and your country if you participate in a civil protest.   III (SS 310)

Suggest ways that TV could affect a person's family life and his education.   II (LA 455)

Explain the difference between a TV viewer who controls his viewing and one who is controlled by it.   II (LA 460)

Watch ten different TV programs. Evaluate each program using the following criteria.   VI (LA 465)
1. Was there violence in the program?
2. Was there a social message in the program? What was it?
3. Was there a message of personal value in the program? What was it?
4. Was there evidence of prejudicial attitudes in the program? What was the situation?
5. Did the program contribute to your intellectual growth?
6. Was the program primarily an escape from reality?

Explain why the following types of TV programs often include violence: (1) news, and (2) movies and series, including detective, spy, western, war, horror, and science-fiction formats.   II

Using the mass media as resources, suggest reasons for two or more viewpoints on a controversial social issue.   II (LA 465)

Describe three advantages of listening to different, conflicting points of view.   II (SS 425)

In a discussion or a written paragraph cite different values or customs in American society. Suggest ways in which individuals with these different values or customs can solve problems cooperatively without conflict.   III (SS 400)

SOCIAL STUDIES INQUIRY SKILLS

SS 425   Analyze statements on the basis of clarity, bias, assumptions, generalizations, and conclusions.   IV (LA 465)

Analyze information to decide if it is relevant to a given problem. Criteria should include (1) pertinence to defining the problem or its causes or solutions; (2) accuracy; (3) cost; and (4) time delay in getting information. (Problem topics: communication, transportation, human resources, human relations, natural resources.)   IV

Recognize an example of an opinion on a current event.   II

Given two passages about the same subject, discuss the following. III
1. The statements that are the same, or nearly the same, in both passages.
2. The statements that are in one passage but not in the other.
3. The statements in one passage that disagree with statements in the other passage.

Collect statements about individuals of different religions, ethnic groups or social groups from news articles, books, conversations with friends. Analyze the statements using these criteria: (1) recognize unstated assumptions; (2) distinguish facts from hypotheses or normative statements, and (3) distinguish conclusions from statements which support them.   IV

Analyze statements concerning the purpose for cities, inferring the writer's bias.   IV

Describe three advantages of listening to different points of view. II

Use the following criteria to differentiate between objective writing and editorial writing.   IV

Editorial Writing	*Objective Writing*
The writer attempts to change opinion.	The writer attempts to take no particular side while writing about a problem.
The writer takes a specific point of view.	The writer attempts to state all possible facts and solutions pertaining to a problem.

69

Develop a list of criteria that would aid in determining whether a written, oral, or visual communication is meant to bring about an emotional response or to convey information.   V

After interviewing a businessman, a student, and a social worker on a particular controversial issue, write a short summary of each position on the issue.   III

Given a resolution about a problem, analyze the content by selecting words that need further definition.   IV

Differentiate between premises and conclusions in loosely organized written passages.   IV

When presented with a major viewpoint and its source, analyze probable causes of bias leading to this viewpoint.   IV

Given an explanation or analysis of some problem or happening, suggest important facts or considerations that may have been omitted in making the explanation or analysis.   II

Using the mass media as resources, analyze two or more viewpoints on a controversial issue.   IV (LA 455)

From a TV, radio, billboard, or magazine advertisement, differentiate between information that is implied and information that is stated.   IV (LA 470)

From a TV, radio, billboard, or magazine advertisement, recognize information that is misleading and explain why it is misleading.   II (LA 470)

Recognize the following signs of bias in a taped radio newscast: loaded words, exaggeration, statements of opinion or statements of prediction presented as fact.   II (LA 200)

Listen to a talk and list the points that should be questioned for supporting evidence.   I (LA 200)

SOCIAL STUDIES

INTERMEDIATE

SS 430 Demonstrate your skills in social studies research by choosing a topic, using appropriate sources of information, organizing the information, and writing or presenting a report. Use a topic from any of the major social studies subjects. III (LA 345)

Given a reading selection and a specific topic, recognize words, phrases, or sentences that are relevant to the topic. II

Given a paragraph and a topic, recognize the topic sentence of the paragraph. II

Given a short selection with the topic stated, recognize supporting details from a list. II

Given a book containing the following parts, locate each part and identify the page number where each appears: an index, a table of contents, a list of illustrations, a bibliography, and a title page. I

Given a topic, locate it in the index of an encyclopedia. I

Using subheadings in an encyclopedia, locate specific information. I

Given a list of topics to be found in an encyclopedia, use guide words in locating the topics. II

Using cross-references in an encyclopedia, locate specific information. I

Demonstrate the ability to use an encyclopedia to find facts about a given subject. II

Given a list of topics and an encyclopedia, an almanac, and an atlas, locate each topic and identify the reference book and the page number where each topic appears. I

Given a list of several sources of recorded information, recognize the sources likely to be helpful in solving a given problem. (Problem topics: natural resources, human resources, communication, transportation, human relations—either within the United States or general to any setting.) II

Given any subject matter topic, demonstrate ability to use the card catalogue to locate and record the topic's call number.   III

Given a list of authors' names, locate them in the card catalogue.   I

Given a list of book titles, locate them in the card catalogue and record their call numbers.   II

Classify evidence from research sources as being either primary or secondary.   II

Identify the characteristics of subjective evidence and the characteristics of objective evidence.   I

Explain what is meant by the term *historical method* and describe how it is used.   II

From your own observations, describe the activities of people involved with solving human problems. (Problem topics: human resources, human relations.)   II

Given a description of the occupations or roles of several people, suggest which people would be likely to have helpful information in dealing with a given problem. (Problem topics: communication, transportation, human resources, human relations, natural resources.)   II

Given a brief statement of a problem and a description of a certain type of resource person, present (orally or in writing) several questions which you would ask about a given problem. (Problem topics: communication, transportation, human resources, human relations, natural resources.)   III

Present an oral report, taking into consideration the following things: (1) the name of the report; (2) a brief introduction; (3) the body of the report; (4) a summary; and (5) use of correct posture, pronunciation, clarity, and tone and delivery.   III

INTERMEDIATE

**SS 435   Demonstrate ability to plan a month-long trip for your family.
III**

> Use reference books, maps and travel folders to find information about Latin American countries which interest you. Use your information to plan an itinerary for an imaginary month-long trip to Latin America for yourself and your family. Describe your reasons for visiting each place.   III

> From a variety of travel folders and brochures, prepare a budget for your family's transportation, food and lodging. Your total budget must not exceed $5000.   III

> Find information on climate and weather conditions in the places you will visit for the appropriate season. Describe the type of clothing you will need to take.   III (SS 345)

> Prepare a list of problems and/or difficult situations your family might encounter on the trip. Describe how each problem might be solved.   III

> Prepare a presentation for your class about your trip. Describe your preparations and illustrate your presentation with pictures of the places you plan to visit.   III (LA 255)

SOCIAL STUDIES

SECONDARY

HISTOry

SS 500 **Demonstrate your ability to combine concepts, principles, and generalizations by developing a hypothesis concerning the history of racial conflict in the United States between the white majority and the black minority.   V (SS 705)**

Identify facts relating to the ancient African empires of Ghana, Mali, and Songhay in the fields of education, government, the arts, economics, the military, slavery, and religion.   I

Describe the effects of the African slave trade on (1) African civilizations, (2) the black man, and (3) European and United States economies.   II

Explain why most white Americans of the pre-Civil War era believed that the black man was inferior.   II

Given a list of statements on the daily conditions of life for the slave in the United States, recognize statements that are supported by evidence.   II

Analyze the attitudes of white society toward slavery and the black man and the effect of these attitudes on the black man, using information about the Haitian Revolution (c. 1800), Denmark Vesey's slave revolt (1822), and Nat Turner's slave revolt (1831).   IV

Explain the effects of abolitionist activity on attitudes in Northern and Southern societies.   II

Support or refute the validity of the following statement, using selected resources as the basis for your conclusion: ''The North went to war against the South primarily to free the black man.''   III

Analyze the following statements to detect logical fallacies.   IV
1. The black man has improved status in this decade.
2. Black people are innately inferior to white people.

Find out how the Reconstruction plans for the freedman that are associated with Abraham Lincoln/Andrew Johnson compare with those associated with Thaddeus Stevens/Charles Sumner. Develop a plan for Reconstruction that you think would have been best to institute in the South after the Civil War.   V (SS 710)

75

Describe the attitudes of the following groups toward the Lincoln/ Johnson and Sumner/Stevens Reconstruction programs: (1) Black Southerners, (2) Anti-Reconstruction Southerners, (3) Northern radicals, and (4) Northern moderates and conservatives. II

Describe post-Reconstruction conditions in the North and South which show that the black man was still viewed as an inferior citizen. II

In a two-page essay compare and contrast the ideas of Booker T. Washington and W.E.B. DuBois on the role that the black man should take in achieving equality in American society. Decide which person's ideas you favor. VI

Describe examples of black contributions to American war efforts since 1870. II

Recognize the methods by which the following African nations achieved independence: Ghana, Nigeria, Kenya, Tanganyika, Rhodesia, Zambia, and Algeria. II

Evaluate the effectiveness of three methods used by a minority group in the United States to improve its environment. VI

Analyze a recent statement made to the mass media to determine the speaker's attitude toward minority groups and equal opportunity. IV (LA 690)

Determine the status of black people in the 20th century in the following areas: (1) employment, (2) education, and (3) housing. In each area consider the inequities for the black man that have been present since 1954. IV

Match the following groups and organizations with a statement that correctly describes the stated position of that group or organization on social change for the Negro. I
1. Black militants
2. Urban League
3. NAACP
4. Southern Christian Leadership Conference
5. John Birch Society
6. Ku Klux Klan

SECONDARY

Analyze the following statement on the basis of social, legal, and economic conditions that have characterized the status of the Negro in the United States: "The Negro in America has been subject to a system designed to destroy his ambition, to prevent his independence, and to cause him to wonder if he really exists at all."   IV

From lists of stated conflicts, suggest reasons for the Supreme Court's desegregation decision in the case of *Brown* v. *Board of Education* (1954) and for the political/moral conflict that has arisen from this decision.   II

For each of the areas listed, suggest one example of a development (since 1946) that led to a rise in the status of Negroes as a group.   II

1. Athletics
2. Government
3. Education
4. Entertainment
5. Ethnic identification
6. Business
7. Political awareness

Describe the American Negro's problem of double identity and explain how at least one black writer has dealt with it.   II (LA 655)

From your reading and from other observations (photos, television, films, records), recognize at least four specific examples of how blacks have used the weapons of humor or creativity against racialism and indifference.   II (LA 655)

Find five examples from poetry or prose by black writers that clearly negate the concept of the Negro as a stereotype.   II (LA 655)

Recognize three distinct evolutionary periods in Malcolm X's life; then give at least one example of awareness or insight that Malcolm X gained in each period.   II (LA 655)

Recognize at least three examples from *The Autobiography of Malcolm X* that illustrate why Malcolm X felt the black man has been robbed of his identity in America.   II (LA 655)

Tell how Malcolm X's account of his childhood experiences compares with an account of an individual's childhood in a different minority group living in America. List the similarities and differences in their experiences.   II (LA 655)

Write a paper or produce a tape developing an incident or a quotation from *The Autobiography of Malcolm X* that you found relevant to yourself or to your society. V (LA 655)

SS 505 Make a judgment on the required study of early civilizations using these criteria: (1) inherent value of acquiring knowledge, (2) relation to understanding of human nature, (3) relation to resolving present-day conflicts, and (4) appreciation of human endeavors. VI

Define each of the following words: *prehistoric, civilization, early civilization,* and *society.* I

In the following list of items, recognize those that were essential to all early civilizations and those not essential. II
1. Clothing
2. Food
3. Machines
4. Water
5. Fire
6. Weapons
7. Tools

On a time line with 3000 B.C. at one end and A.D. 2000 at the other end, label the beginning and end of each of these time periods. I
1. Egyptian before the Hyksos Dynasty
2. Early Chinese "Hwang Ho—Yellow River"
3. Incan civilization
4. Mayan civilization
5. Aztec civilization
6. Ancient Greek civilization
7. Ancient Hebrew civilization
8. Ancient Roman civilization

Identify the geographic location and cultural contributions of Aryan, Aztec, Dravidian, Egyptian, Greek, Hsian, Inca, Phoenician, and Sumerian civilizations. Classify contributions involving religion and government. II

Based on speculations about the reasons for migration of early men and civilization from one continent to another, develop your own logical explanations, stating your rationale. V

Develop a plan and make tentative work assignments for a staff of five archaeological assistants who, under your direction, might excavate and interpret the significance of an archaeological site you may choose. V

SECONDARY

Compare and contrast two dynasties in early Chinese civilization on the basis of art, education, scientific advancement, and government. VI

Develop a hypothesis for the rise and fall of civilizations, using information about the early civilizations as evidence. V (SS 715)

Describe principles that must be accepted in order to form a government. II

On a time line identify the century of the greatest expansion of the Greek Empire and the century of the greatest expansion of the Roman Empire. I

Classify the following governmental bases as Greek or early Roman: (1) the Senate, (2) Delphic Oracle, (3) Law of the Twelve Tables, (4) Law of Nations. II (SS 590)

From the list below, recognize the characteristics of government in early Rome that were different from those in Athens, Sparta, or Alexandria and explain the differences. II (SS 590)
1. Private schools   4. Republic
2. Slavery   5. Religion
3. Written laws

Identify a major accomplishment of the following politically active men: Livy, Tacitus, Julius Caesar, Herodotus, Plato, Socrates, Homer, Aristotle, Demosthenes, Alexander, Xenophon, Thucydides, Hannibal, Marcus Aurelius, and Cicero. I (SS 590)

SS 510 Make judgments on statements that indicate the contributions of Renaissance and non-Western medieval cultures to present society. VI

In a group, discuss the characteristics of the Dark Ages that contributed to the development of feudalism in Europe. III

Participate in a short discussion of one of the following socio-economic systems of feudalistic society: agriculture, law, caste system, and defense. III

Explain five ways the Church in the Middle Ages helped fill the roles now performed by central governments. II

Recognize the socio-economic reforms of the Crusades that helped revive towns and trade in Europe.   II

Describe the guild system of the later Middle Ages.   II

Compare and contrast characteristics of the medieval town and the contemporary town and evaluate them according to how well they fulfill the needs of their respective times.   VI

Recognize eight achievements attributed to the Moslems of the Middle Ages.   II

Compare and contrast the major political, social, economic, and cultural systems of the Byzantine Empire and Western Europe during the Middle Ages.   VI

Compare and contrast feudalism in Europe and feudalism in Asia, evaluating the systems according to how effectively they met the needs of their societies.   VI

Explain why Mohammedanism spread so rapidly in its first 300 years in comparison with Christianity.   II

Identify four differences between the European medieval and Renaissance eras.   I

Briefly summarize the major accomplishments of at least five European Renaissance figures (such as Dante, Chaucer, Erasmus, and Michelangelo).   II

Present evidence to support or refute the argument that the Renaissance began in Northern Italy and later spread to the rest of Europe. III

Write three to five paragraphs in which you support or reject this statement: "The so-called European Renaissance has an unknown beginning and has not ended."   III (LA 547)

Compare and contrast three examples of disunity in the Catholic Church between A.D. 1000 and A.D. 1500 with three examples of disunity that presently exist.   VI

SECONDARY

Match the following names with each man's philosophic attitude and major accomplishment: Calvin, Henry VIII (England), Huss, Luther, and Wycliffe. I

Explain, using at least three examples, how the Catholic Church attempted to block the Protestant Reformation. II

Put the following time periods in chronological order according to their approximate dates: Age of Imperialism, Middle Ages, Age of Reason (Enlightenment), and the Renaissance. II

SS 515   Make judgments on statements that indicate the contributions the Industrial Revolution has made to 20th-century political movements and economic organizations.   VI

Predict three problems a nation now beginning to industrialize might have. Base your prediction on characteristics of early stages of industrialization and on the history of early English industrial development. III

Using information from literature (in written, film or tape form), discuss the living and working conditions of the early factory system (18th and 19th centuries). III (LA 650)

Classify by author written interpretations of the ideas of Thomas Malthus, David Ricardo, and Adam Smith. II

Using fifty-year intervals on a time line that includes A.D. 1700–2000, identify the times when each of the following countries became highly industrialized: China, England, France, Japan, United States, U.S.S.R., and two others of your choice. I

Explain the social, economic and political causes of the "commercial revolution" and, in the same terms, explain the major changes brought about by the revolution before 1800. II

Apply generalizations about two political, two social, and two economic results of the Industrial Revolution to current situations. III

In three paragraphs, describe a given invention as (1) several inventions combined, (2) the result of earlier inventions, and (3) likely to cause another invention. III (LA 545)

Identify accurate descriptions of each of the following types of economies: capitalistic, communistic, socialistic, and mixed-market economies. I (SS 670)

Classify three criticisms raised by 19th-century social novelists under one or more of the following categories: economic, political, or social criticism. II (LA 635)

Summarize the major social contributions of each of the following men: Charles Fourier, Robert Owen, and Claude Saint-Simon. II

Write three paragraphs about capitalism. In each paragraph describe a practice of capitalism that Marx criticized and that was modified by the capitalistic system itself. III (LA 545)

Write a paper or give a talk outlining three effects of the Industrial Revolution in Europe on Asia, Africa, and South America. III (LA 515, LA 547)

SS 520 Show that you can participate in a debate involving the historical significance of a current issue in your state. III (LA 525)

Given a problem faced by the pioneers of your state, identify a natural resource that helped solve the problem and tell how it did so. I

List in chronological order the major historical events of your state from its period as an unsettled wilderness to the present. I

Recognize the economic resources presently found in your state. II (SS 665)

Describe the role your state plays in educating youth. II (SS 675)

Summarize arguments delivered by politicians and private citizens in your state regarding the state budget and responsibilities to the people. II (SS 675)

Present a report on the greatest problem your state faces today, including a description of any current attempts to solve the problem. III (SS 665, LA 547)

SOCIOLOGY and anThropOLOGY

SS 525 **Show that you can support or refute the prediction that a period of racial conflict will precede a period of racial equality and peaceful coexistence. III**

Identify one group of people in the United States who represent a minority in each of the following respects: (1) language, (2) national background, (3) religious faith, (4) political ideologies, (5) physical appearance, (6) economic theories, and (7) social beliefs. I

Recognize definitions of each of the following terms often used in reference to minority groups and recognize examples of each term: (1) prejudice, (2) stereotype, (3) discrimination, (4) bigotry, (5) racism, and (6) intolerance. II (SS 705)

Given a list of statements describing group relationships, recognize those that show prejudice and those that do not. II (SS 705)

Given a list of "prejudicial statements," make inferences on the basis of the author's prejudice in each case: (1) fear, (2) greed, or (3) ignorance. IV (SS 705, LA 695)

Given four specific values held by the majority of Americans, analyze the motives behind statements made by members of the majority groups about behaviors of minority groups. IV

Describe four recent situations—two racial and two religious—in which minorities have been the targets of discrimination in the United States. II

Write an essay of no more than one page describing situations in which you are in a minority and situations in which you are in a majority. III (LA 547)

Present a hypothesis to explain why some whites hold racist beliefs and, based on your hypothesis, suggest three ways to reduce racist attitudes. III (SS 715)

Predict the significance of Black Power in our society in relation to the following areas of reform.   III
1. Business responsibilities for blacks
2. Political and social activities
3. Black man's self-image
4. Leadership of the black community
5. New questions and demands presented to the white community

In an essay, compare and evaluate the predictions of Martin Luther King, Jr., and Malcolm X on the future of black-white relations in American society.   VI (LA 655)

Analyze the methods used by Martin Luther King's nonviolence movement and determine whether they were consistent with the following statement: "Each time a man stands up for an idea, or acts to improve the lot of others, or strikes out against injustice, he sends forth a tiny ripple of hope."—Robert F. Kennedy   IV

Given statements advocating integration, separatism, and segregation of the black man in America, support one position.   III

Describe five basic causes of racial disorders, using a published report such as the Kerner Report and citing your source.   II

Write a research paper on the contemporary problems of Indians in our culture, including information on the policy of the federal government toward the Indians, contributions of Indians to American society, and attitudes held by the racial majority. Use information from all media, library sources, and interviews if possible.   III (LA 560)

SS 530   By forming generalizations, demonstrate your ability to perceive reasons for cultural differences among peoples of the world.   IV

Read about persons of another culture and describe five of their cultural attitudes or customs. Then offer explanations for the existence of these attitudes or customs. Cite the source for your examples.   II (LA 650)

Recognize some attitudes, stereotypes, or biases about people of another cultural, racial, or ethnic group. Be able to cite examples from movies, literature, or personal experience that reinforce or modify the attitude, stereotype, or bias.   II (LA 650)

SECONDARY

Demonstrate that people of various cultures often express identical emotions. A set of pictures forming a collage, a set of film clips, or a set of audio tape sequences would be an appropriate demonstration. III (LA 650)

Describe at least six instances in which practices disapproved of by one culture are acceptable in another culture. Cite your sources. II (SS 710)

Discuss at least three ways in which geography and ecology have affected culture. III (SS 650)

Describe cultural practices of three countries, some of which are determined by geography, some of which are not. II

Recognize two examples that indicate that a culture has retained practices that probably originated under different geographical conditions. II (SS 650)

SS 535 Demonstrate your ability to combine concepts, principles, and generalizations by proposing solutions to problems produced for individuals by advancing technology. V (SS 665)

Given a list of man's inventions and activities that affect his environment, review for each invention and activity the benefits and harms that have resulted. II (SC 590)

Pretend you wish to construct a machine. Design the machine and list the materials you would need to build it—without help from another person. V

Given photographs, recognize three technological societies. II

Using pictures of architectural accomplishments in nine societies, explain which pictures you think depict a high level of technological development and which depict a lower level. II

Analyze the disintegration of three ancient technological societies from the following list and identify three technological innovations that could have prevented or slowed each society's disintegration: Mohenjo Daro, India; Angkor Wat, Cambodia; Crete, Greece; Etruscan Italy; Chichen Itza, Yucatan, Mexico; Teotihuacan, Mexico; Machu Picchu, Peru; ancient Egypt; ancient Babylonia; ancient Ur. IV

From several photographs, identify early Egyptian artifacts that were carried to other nations to symbolize the conquest or control of Egypt. I

Using words and/or pictures, trace the development of one modern tool back to its probable origin or simplest form. II

In three paragraphs, describe one technological innovation in common use in technological societies since 2000 B.C., one found in societies before A.D. 1600 but rarely since, and one unique to 20th-century societies. II

Analyze in an informal debate the pros and cons of technological society. IV (LA 525)

Discuss apparent values in a given society that cause corruption or make some people victims of their society. III

Explain the extent to which technological progress is related to the destruction of man's natural environment. Give specific examples to support your answer. II (SC 590)

Explain the consequences of technological progress on given values of the first half of the 20th century. II

Debate the issue of support for the large, mechanized farm vs. support for the small, family farm. IV

Define the term *automation,* and list five beneficial effects of automation on society. I

Discuss five developments which characterize the Age of Automation, and determine whether each development supports or does not support the following statement: "We live in an age of automation in which society functions like a machine and men like its parts; man as a cog in the production machine is becoming less and less an individual who thinks for himself and more and more controlled by the rhythm and demands of the machine." III

Recognize four ways in which a central data system poses a threat to personal privacy. II

SECONDARY

Develop a plan to enable people in the Age of Automation to maintain their role as individuals.   V (SS 695)

Present a panel discussion on the elimination of jobs by technology. Consider what is being done or should be done to create new jobs. (Use documented information in your discussion.)   III (LA 525, SS 710)

SS 540   Demonstrate your ability to combine concepts, principles, and generalizations by developing a campaign to educate the members of your community about local ecology problems. Your campaign should include materials for all age groups and work groups. Provide for implementation of resource protection devices.   V (SC 590)

List similar and different problems encountered by United States and Soviet government agencies in coping with environmental pollution.   I

Present legal, financial, and physical evidence to support or refute this statement: "Laws that stress the prevention of pollution are usually more effective than those that insist on correction."   III (SC 590, SS 710)

Draw a political cartoon showing your viewpoint on the following issue: "Rapid industrial growth is (is not) a major obstacle to long-range conservationist efforts."   III

Develop a two-page recommendation or a 5-minute oral presentation for preserving man's natural environment consistent with the principles of social economics and with the concept of "the least harm to the least number".   IV (SS 665)

Present an appropriate solution for three conservation problems. III (SC 590)

SS 545   Demonstrate your ability to combine concepts, principles, and generalizations by writing a paper that explains the need for social change in the area of women's rights.   V (SS 715)

Find and use information to support these assumptions about each topic listed: boys and girls are taught to act differently; different

values are taught boys and girls; changes are taking place in values being accepted by boys and girls.   III
1. Showing emotion
2. Aggression
3. Manners (in grade school)
4. Manners (in high school and dating)
5. Personal appearance
6. Physical activity
7. Art, music, and dancing

Using labor statistics on employment opportunities and data on state restrictions for women, write an essay telling your viewpoints on the issue of equal opportunity and status for women.   V (SS 655)

Using specific persons and their achievements as well as general examples, explain five ways that women influence decisions in each of the following areas: (1) economics, (2) politics, and (3) cultural activities.   II

Discuss similarities and differences between the black revolution and the female revolution in the present century by identifying limitations and advances made by each revolution in the following areas: (1) voting rights, (2) education, (3) employment, and (4) politics.   III (LA 655, LA 660)

Write a two-page essay in which you compare the typical roles of black women and white women in American society by answering the following questions.   VI (LA 655, LA 660)
1. What differences are there between black and white women in the amount and kind of influence they have in the home?
2. What differences are there in employment and economic influence between typical black women and typical white women?
3. What differences are there in education and educational influence between typical black women and typical white women?
4. What changes, if any, are taking place in the typical role of black women and of white women?

Having accurately described a specific social injustice involving women's rights, write a piece of legislation directed toward the correction of the injustice.   V

Develop a proposal offering a plausible solution for each of three problems faced by minority groups in the United States.   V

SECONDARY

SS 550   Given five urban problems, make judgments on suggested solutions.   VI (SS 665)

Identify five economic characteristics of an industrial society that do not exist in a nonindustrial society.   I (SS 665)

Define the following terms associated with the growth of cities and urban problems.   I (SS 665)

1. Urban
2. Suburban
3. Urban sprawl
4. Depressed areas
5. Slum
6. Ghetto
7. Slum lord
8. Absentee landlord
9. City planning
10. Redevelopment
11. Zoning
12. Tenement
13. Mores
14. Minority groups
15. Ethnocentrism

From documented data, form generalizations about three causes of urban growth.   IV

Identify three results of industrialization in the United States during the 20th century.   I

Recognize at least one area in the United States that will be a megalopolis by the year 2000 and explain why this will occur.   II

Review reasons and evidence that social change is affected by variations in migration patterns into the urban areas.   I

Review the activities that take place in each of the following kinds of urban zones: the central business district, the periphery of the central business district, a zone in transition, a new residential suburb.   I

Discuss causes of slums and ghettos. Support with factual evidence one of the solutions offered by sociologists or politicians for the problems of slums and ghettos.   III (SS 660)

Recognize problems that are associated with slum-clearance projects and urban redevelopment.   II (SS 660)

Develop a plan for a slum-clearance project that resolves the major difficulties associated with such projects.   V (SS 660)

POLITICaL science

SS 555 **Show that you can support or refute the following statement: "The United States Constitution was written as a guide for all times. Changing it or interpreting it within the context of new attitudes or beliefs violates the intent of our founding fathers." III**

Identify ten legislative powers and five executive powers given in Articles I and II of the United States Constitution. I

Recognize examples of the use of three powers, constitutional or nonconstitutional, of the legislative branch which check powers of the executive branch. II

Identify three powers, constitutional or nonconstitutional, of the executive branch which check powers of the legislative branch. I

Given incidents involving conflict between the executive branch and the legislature, recognize the potential point or points of conflict between executive functions and legislative functions in each incident. II

Given hypothetical political situations, predict conflicts between the executive function and the legislative function. III

Using research techniques, summarize the history of one executive-legislative conflict. II (SS 710)

List the constitutional and nonconstitutional powers possessed by the president that are legislative, executive, judicial, diplomatic, or military in nature. I

Recognize examples of four ways in which a United States president has served as "Chief Legislator" and two ways which he has served as "Chief Executive." II

Given a series of presidential decisions showing various uses of presidential powers by different presidents, recognize the constitutional or nonconstitutional power that each president exercised in each case in arriving at that decision. II

SECONDARY

Given various historical and hypothetical actions of United States presidents, recognize whether the action taken is indicative of a broad interpretation of presidential power or whether it is indicative of an action which would be acceptable to both a broad and a strict interpretation of presidential power.   II

Present evidence either for or against this statement: "Roosevelt's attempt to 'pack' the Supreme Court in 1937 was ill-conceived, ill-timed, poorly executed, and ill-fated in the long run."   III (SS 705)

List five political or historical developments that account for the increase in presidential power in the 20th century.   I

Give at least five examples to explain how the interpretation of the federal government's power to tax has changed since the United States Constitution was written.   II

Given a list of five ways that the United States Constitution changes, name a specific historic example for each item on the list.   I

Given a written selection concerning various constitutional rights, recognize the specific constitutional rights involved.   II

Describe instances of specific constitutional rights in conflict with other constitutional rights.   II

Write an essay based on research on one of the following topics.   V (LA 547, SS 705)
1. Should the Supreme Court have complete authority to decide the meaning of the Constitution?
2. Why is it necessary for the Constitution to be flexible? Give examples.

Write an essay in which you support or refute Thomas Jefferson's recommendation that each branch of government should have the exclusive right to judge the constitutionality of its own actions.   V (LA 547, SS 705)

SS 560   Show your understanding of the forms and functions of our government by matching listed problems to the branch of government most directly involved in their solution.   II

Classify governmental powers as federal, state, or concurrent powers.   II

List the names of the following federal, state, and local elected representatives from your area. I
1. The two United States senators
2. The United States representative
3. The state senator
4. The state representative
5. The governor
6. Three local officials

Given the steps necessary for an idea to become a law at the federal level, list them in proper sequence. I

Identify the major rules and procedures that apply to floor action in the national Senate and those that apply to floor action in the national House of Representatives. I

Match the following seven federal regulatory agencies with their functions: Federal Power Commission, Federal Trade Commission, Securities and Exchange Commission, Federal Communications Commission, Federal Reserve Board, National Labor Relations Board, and Interstate Commerce Commission. I

Recognize statements which illustrate two advantages and two disadvantages of governments with power centered in a legislature and of governments with power centered in an executive. II

Describe five duties of the president that are specified in the United States Constitution by summarizing news reports of a president carrying out these duties. II

List the constitutional and nonconstitutional powers possessed by the president that are legislative, executive, judicial, diplomatic, or military in nature. I

Evaluate a legal or governmental practice followed in your state before it gained statehood. VI

List three powers most state governors have. I

Represent on a chart the structure and jurisdiction of the federal court and your state court systems. II

Describe three types of municipal governments. II

SECONDARY

SS 565 **Make judgments on the judicial system in the United States using these criteria: (1) method of selecting the jury, (2) methods of selecting the judges, (3) use of bail for retaining suspects, and (4) past and present judicial decisions reported in mass media.   VI**

Identify the duties of each of the five following court officers: the Public Defender, the judge, the District Attorney, the bailiff, and the Clerk of the Court.   I

Recognize accurate descriptions of the following procedures in a typical criminal case in the United States judicial system.   II
1. Investigation
2. Arrest
3. Initial appearance before a magistrate
4. Making formal charges of crime (indictment)
5. Arraignment and trial
6. Punishment
7. Process of appeal

Write a report of an imaginary court proceeding which includes the following elements of a typical civil case in the United States judicial system.   V (LA 680)
1. Major participants in the court and the responsibilities of those participants
2. Who decides whether a rule has been violated and how it is decided
3. What action the court may take on proven rule violators

Discuss the following aspects of the Supreme Court decisions in *Plessy* v. *Ferguson* and *Brown* v. *Board of Education of Topeka.* III
1. How court decisions reflect currents of social change and social thought
2. How courts form law as well as follow law
3. How court decisions can create new issues as they resolve old ones

SS 570 **Make judgments on the effectiveness of protection of individual rights in the United States.   VI**

Describe specific constitutional safeguards that protect individuals in given situations.   II

Identify the rights guaranteed to the individual in the first ten amendments to the United States Constitution and give an example of each right.   I

Predict a conflict which might arise between protecting the rights of the accused and the pursuit of justice as a result of the decisions of the Supreme Court in the cases of *Escobedo* v. *Illinois* and *Miranda* v. *Arizona.*   III

Given case histories and court decisions involving the right of a person not to testify against himself, discuss one reason why the principle preventing compulsory self-incrimination is necessary and one reason why it produces problems in the pursuit of justice.   III

Given case histories and court decisions from cases involving "unreasonable search and seizure," discuss the conflict between the rights of an individual and the needs of society.   III (SS 705)

Using statistical evidence from sources in the United States, England, and Japan, support or refute legislation regulating the sale of guns in the United States.   III (SS 705)

Describe three responsibilities of an individual that are important in protecting individual rights in a democracy.   II (SS 725)

In a paragraph for each, describe five types of legal situations in which a teenager could become involved.   II

Discuss the status of juveniles on the basis of (1) safeguards from publicity, (2) support from legal aid, and (3) protection from prejudiced judgments.   III

SS 575   Make judgments on the effectiveness of provisions in our government that allow individuals to influence decisions.   VI

Explain whether or not the following are essential elements for a fair election in the United States: (1) choice of candidates, (2) 100% participation of registered voters, (3) secret ballot, (4) a judicial system that protects an individual, and (5) party caucus.   II

SECONDARY

Given statements about voting behavior (frequency, socioeconomic distribution, age distribution) and voter qualifications, recognize those that describe voting behavior in the United States most accurately. II

Describe the procedure for electing a president of the United States according to the Constitution. II

Analyze election returns from the past three presidential elections to determine why cities and urban voters have become important in American politics. IV (SS 710)

Recognize statements which describe the following characteristics of political parties in the United States: (1) main goals, (2) main interests represented by major parties, (3) local, state, and national organization, and (4) main functions. II

Use specific case studies to support your positions on the following issues. III
1. Special interest groups do or do not effectively represent public opinion.
2. Special interest groups do or do not effectively influence decision makers to respond to public opinion.

Explain five forces influencing the legislative process in your state and nation. II

Define the term *lobbyist* in relation to Congress. Identify the advantages and disadvantages of lobbying as a major influence on the legislative process. I

Pretend you are a national senator or representative and write or present orally a statement of philosophy defining your position on the following conflicts. III (LA 665)
1. Your responsibility to local vested interests and local public opinion vs. your responsibilities to national interests
2. Your responsibilities to local vested interests and local public opinion vs. personal political convictions

Describe two ways an organized group in the United States can use lobbying and mass demonstrations to influence the decision of an elected representative. II

Classify propaganda statements into one of the following categories: name calling, glaring generality, transfers, testimonials, plain folks, card stacking, and band wagon.   II (LA 695)

Identify three ways in which an individual in the United States can influence the decisions made by his elected representatives.   I

Identify the procedures for amending the United States Constitution.   I

Given a situation in which there is a conflict between the actions of the federal government and the interests of a state, support or refute the following opinions.   III
1. The state's rights have been violated according to the Constitution.
2. The actions taken by the federal government were justifiable because of the nature of the situation.

Write an essay proposing three laws you think would make the United States a better place in which to live and tell why each law is needed.   V

Identify four ways in which the right to dissent may be legally exercised.   I

Recognize situations in which a conflict might arise between the right to dissent and the need to maintain law and order (to safeguard other basic rights).   II

Evaluate "the right to dissent" and other individual rights on the basis of the resulting upheaval such rights may cause, using evidence from current events, history, and philosophy.   VI

In an essay, critically evaluate this statement: "To break the law of the land is always serious but it is not always wrong." In your evaluation, consider the following questions.   VI
1. What is meant by civil disobedience?
2. What are some limitations of civil disobedience?
3. Give an example of a law which you consider unjust. Explain.
4. Do you agree with the quoted statement? Why or why not?
5. Why must a person who disobeys a law that he considers morally wrong be expected to pay the consequences for disobeying that law?

SECONDARY

List two social, two economic, and two political causes of the Progressive Movement in the United States from 1900 to 1917. I

List at least ten major political, economic, and social leaders of the Progressive Movement from 1900 to 1917, and indicate the particular contribution that each made to the movement. I

Discuss five social, political, or economic reforms accomplished by the Progressive Movement. Support each reform in terms of its contemporary historical importance, using evidence from social research. III

Identify five possible causes for the decline of the Progressive Movement in the 1920s. I

SS 580 **Show your understanding of cause and effect in political interaction by explaining the origins and results of a political event of your choice. II (SS 705)**

Describe principles that must be accepted in order to form a government. II

Prepare at least three analytical questions to guide the study of a society's political system. III

Given a case study of political interaction, recognize the following elements: (1) the political issues, (2) the sources of the political issues, (3) the political techniques used by the people, (4) the political resources of the people, and (5) the policy decisions. II

Describe how the following agents socialize political attitudes and behaviors and explain what political attitudes and/or behaviors you have learned from these agents: (1) family unit, (2) formal educational institutions, (3) peer groups, (4) employment situations, (5) mass media, (6) direct contacts with the political system. II

Given a list of various interpretations of qualities an ideal citizen should have, explain why three of them would or would not be in the best interest of the United States. II

SS 585 **Show that you can discuss the democratic ideals expressed by 18th-century writers as they are implemented today in two countries. III (LA 660)**

List at least five political characteristics found in almost all democratic societies. I

Identify the following English documents. I
1. Document that limits the power of England's House of Lords
2. Document that first limited the power of English kings
3. Document that grants English middle class voting rights
4. Document that guarantees the most rights to most Englishmen
5. Document that establishes the practice of trial by jury

Identify the contribution to English democracy made by each of the following Englishmen: Robert Walpole, Benjamin Disraeli, Oliver Cromwell, and John Locke. I

From a list of provisions that have their roots in English law, recognize those which have been incorporated into the United States Constitution. II

Identify six major political concepts defining the roles of the government and the individual in the United States democratic process that have their roots in the British political system. I

Recognize any three statements of philosophy drawn from the writings of Thomas Jefferson, Alexis de Tocqueville, John Stuart Mill, and Edmund Burke, and from the U.S. Constitution and contemporary sayings. Explain why you feel each quotation selected corresponds or conflicts with the Anglo-American democratic heritage. II

Identify conditions that correctly describe aspects of the "Old Regime" in France that led to the French Revolution. I

Identify the major works of Voltaire, Rousseau, Montesquieu, and Adam Smith and identify one idea of each philosopher that helped lay the groundwork for the French Revolution. I

Identify the democratic reforms that were a result of the French Revolution. I

Identify reforms that were instituted by Napoleon and affected the rest of Europe. I

SECONDARY

Recognize the major political results of each of the three French revolutions. II

Describe the British Parliament and the French Fifth Republic's government, using the following questions as a guide. II
1. How many houses or political bodies are there in each government?
2. Who is eligible to vote?
3. Is there a formal written constitution?
4. How many major political parties exist in each country?
5. How do the president and the prime minister obtain office?
6. Does the system of justice include a trial by jury?
7. What is the role of the individual citizen in each?

Answer the following questions about Charles de Gaulle and Napoleon. I
1. How did each become popular?
2. How did each obtain office?
3. What was the attitude of each toward England?
4. What was the attitude of each toward nationalism?

SS 590 Show that you can support or refute the value of contributions made by Roman law, Greek democracy, and Judeo-Christian ethics to the social-political structure of Western civilization. III (SS 505)

On a time line, identify the century of the greatest expansion of the Greek Empire and the century of the greatest expansion of the Roman Empire. I

Classify the following governmental bases as Greek or early Roman: (1) the Senate, (2) Delphic Oracle, (3) Law of the Twelve Tables, (4) Law of Nations. II

From the list below, recognize the characteristics of government in early Rome that were different from those in Athens, Sparta, or Alexandria, and explain the differences. II
1. Private schools   4. Republic
2. Slavery   5. Religion
3. Written laws

Identify a major political accomplisnment of the following men: Livy, Tacitus, Julius Caesar, Herodotus, Plato, Socrates, Homer, Aristotle, Demosthenes, Alexander, Xenophon, Thucydides, Hannibal, Marcus Aurelius, and Cicero. I

Write three paragraphs describing how Roman law, Greek democracy, and Judeo-Christian ethics are important ideas basic to Western civilization. III

SS 595 Demonstrate your ability to combine concepts, principles, and generalizations by developing an outline for a national governmental structure that, in your opinion, is ideal. V (SS 710)

Given a list of political characteristics, classify them as either democratic or totalitarian. II

Write a two-page report comparing the advantages and disadvantages of democratic and totalitarian societies. III (LA 547)

Given a list of structural and functional characteristics, recognize those which describe modern governmental bureaucracies. II

SS 600 By forming generalizations about a given world crisis, demonstrate your ability to perceive causes of international conflict. IV

Identify three conditions that hindered German unification before 1850 and three conditions that hindered Italian unification before 1850. I

Describe the conditions that tended to unite the German people and those that tended to unite the Italian people just prior to the unification of each nation. II

Represent on a time line five 19th-century events that led to the unification of Germany or Italy. II

Given descriptions of the role played by three leaders of Italian unification and three leaders of German unification, match the name of each leader to the description of his role. I

Analyze briefly similarities between the unifications of Germany and Italy. IV

SECONDARY

Describe five policies followed by Bismarck after Germany became unified and the ramifications of these policies. II

Identify two nationalistic movements from 1815–1920 and name the political units each created and destroyed. I

Describe the militarism in the 20th-century history of Africa, Asia, Australia, Europe, North America, Pacifica, and South America. II

Giving examples, explain how each of the following helped to cause World War I: militarism, alliances, nationalism, and imperialism. II

Identify five provisions of the Treaty of Versailles. I

Explain how three European nations were created between 1915 and 1939. II

List five 20th-century examples of each of the following: military force used in an attempt to achieve internal goals and military force used to achieve international goals. I

Identify seven inventions that have made warfare in the 20th century deadlier. I

Represent on a time line ten events of the 20th century that helped to bring on World War II. II

Prepare an argument for or against continued support of the military powers in the United States. Present your arguments to someone with opposing views and discuss the differences. III

Given a list of examples classify them as economic, political, social, or military causes of imperialism. II

For each of three of the following forms of imperialism, recognize an appropriate definition and an example of annexation, concession, leasehold, mandate, protectorate, satellite, sphere of influence, and trusteeship. II

Identify three examples of European imperialism in Africa, three in Asia, and three in Central or South America. I

Classify three advantages and three disadvantages of imperialism as economic, political, or social. Identify those which were advantages to the colony. II

List two examples of conflict between imperialist powers in Africa, two in Asia, two in the Balkans, and two in the Middle East between the year 1850 and the present. I

Recognize wartime conditions that were characteristic of each of the following countries in the years 1939 through 1945: Japan, England, France, and the United States. II

Recognize the purposes for organizing the League of Nations and the United Nations and recognize reasons for the successes and/or failures of each in accomplishing these purposes. II

Produce a theory of political control over inter-nation conflicts which might be the basis for a world organization of nations. V

Summarize in one paragraph an international problem reported in a live or recorded news broadcast. II

Given a series of four sentences, recognize the statement that most accurately describes how European colonization affected Africa between 1870 and 1914. II

In a three-page biography, evaluate the political success of one of the following African nationalist leaders: Jomo Kenyatta, Haile Selassie, Abdul Nasser, or William V. Tubman. Include a description of his rise to power and of his personality. VI (LA 570)

Choose an African colony and play two opposing roles: a colonialist and a nationalist leader, both of whom were active in that colony just prior to the time it received its independence. As you play each role, present at least two reasons why you are for or against independence. III

Given a list of descriptive statements about Pan-Africanism in the 1960s, recognize the three most accurate. II

SECONDARY

Describe three economic, political, and social problems which have prevented African nations from achieving economic, political, or social stability. II

Construct a table which contains the following data: the names of all African nations listed in the order in which they achieved political independence, the name of every colony in Africa, and the name of every territory; the form of government (monarchy, democracy, socialism, democratic-socialism, communism, or fascism); the name and official title of African heads of state and the number of years each has served as head of state; the area (in square miles); the population; and a brief description of the economy (mostly agricultural, small farms, Europeanized agricultural, extensive mining, or heavily industrial). III

In one paragraph, define *nationalism* and, in a second paragraph, identify an example of nationalism in Asia. I

Analyze statements from a study of Asian conflict that reflect the author's bias regarding nationalism. IV

Identify the names and locations of at least twenty Asian nations. I

Identify three Asian nations that have not been colonized during the nineteenth or twentieth centuries. I

Put in chronological order three events that led to the independence of each of the following: the Philippines, Cambodia, India, Korea, and Indonesia. II

Choose one Asian nationalist leader and write a biography of no more than three pages describing his rise to power, his personality, and two effects of his leadership on the nation. III

Differentiate between statements which support or reject the following generalization: "China is more nationalistic than communistic and Mao Tse-tung is more capitalistic than communistic." II

Classify the following problems as local, regional, or international (global): (1) a civil war, (2) a conflict among four nations, (3) a dispute between neighboring ranches, (4) a dispute between neighboring states within a nation, and (5) a conflict between two countries. II

Recognize an element of similarity in tactics, ideology, geography, economics, or leadership shared by the historical events paired below. II
1. Attacks of the United States on Spanish Manila (1898) and of Japan on American Pearl Harbor (1941)
2. Establishment of the League of Nations (1920) and of the United Nations (1945)
3. The American and French revolutions
4. The American and Russian revolutions
5. Colonization of Australia and South Africa by Europeans
6. The expansion of Christianity and the expansion of Islam
7. Wars for independence in South America (1800–1821) and in Africa (1945–present)
8. Invasion of Russia by Napoleon and by Hitler

From the following possible causes of war, recognize those that apply to (1) the Spanish-American War, (2) World War I, (3) World War II, (4) Korean War, (5) Vietnam War. II

1. National interest
2. National pride
3. Desire to expand
4. Desire for self-determination
5. Aggression
6. Fear
7. Revenge
8. Economic conflicts
9. Political conflicts
10. Religious conflicts
11. Propaganda
12. Desire to contain

Determine the cultural, political, and social effects of the Spanish-American War, World War I, and the Korean War on the major countries involved. Use these questions as a guide. IV
1. What were the chief material gains, if any, for the major countries involved?
2. What were the material losses, if any, for the major countries involved?
3. What prewar goals, if any, were achieved by the major countries involved?
4. What prewar goals, if any, were *not* achieved by the major countries involved?

From the point of view of the United States, discuss each of the following events, using the concepts of expansion, imperialism, isolationism, containment, intervention, coexistence, and neutrality: (1) Louisiana Purchase (1803), (2) seizure of the Philippines (1898), (3) League of Nations (1919), (4) Spanish Civil War (1936), (5) Korean War (1950), (6) Hungarian Revolt (1956), and (7) Dominican Crisis (1965). III

SECONDARY

Using the concepts of expansion, imperialism, isolationism, containment, intervention, coexistence, and neutrality, explain in two or three sentences how the United States has utilized its power to achieve its objective for each of the following plans and events: (1) Marshall Plan (1947), (2) Berlin Airlift (1948), (3) Korean War (1950), (4) Suez Crisis (1956), (5) Lebanon Invasion (1958), (6) Alliance for Progress (1961), and (7) Cuban Missile Crisis (1962). In your explanation specify the type of power used in each case and the kind of national objective. II

"Critics of our foreign policy have said that our firm stand in Vietnam is precisely the type of commitment that represents an abuse of our power, a squandering of our resources, and a futile and misguided effort to play world policemen." In essay form, critically evaluate the preceding statement, paying special attention to the following questions. VI (LA 547)
1. Have we squandered our resources since the Vietnam War began and, if so, how?
2. What type of commitment do we have in Vietnam?
3. Do you think we are playing "world policemen" in Vietnam?
4. Do you agree or disagree with the above statement?

Present to three fellow students a brief oral background report which will inform them about an international problem. III (LA 515)

Analyze one written or recorded report on an international problem presented by another student and identify extreme statements, unsupported conclusions, and logical conclusions. IV (LA 565)

Recognize at least two examples of conflict in an international problem. II

Using a definition of each of the following terms, explain how each relates to foreign policy: (1) expansion, (2) imperialism, (3) isolationism, (4) containment, (5) intervention, (6) coexistence, and (7) neutrality. II

Present evidence from world history to support or refute this statement: "Too much involvement in foreign affairs over too long a time weakens a nation internally." III (SS 705)

SS 605 Demonstrate your ability to combine concepts, principles, and generalizations by developing a theory of political control over international conflicts which might be the basis for a world organization of nations.   V (SS 715)

Match each of four functions of the League of Nations with the branch of the League of Nations that carried out the function.   I

Describe two examples of the accomplishments and two examples of the failures of the League of Nations and suggest the reasons for the failures.   II

Describe three reasons the League of Nations failed.   II

Evaluate the success of four examples of attempts at formalized international cooperation between 1900 and 1940. Include the factors which contributed to and detracted from the success of each attempt.   VI

Summarize the problems faced by President Wilson in his desire to have a just peace treaty written at the Versailles Conference and give reasons for his apparent willingness to compromise while he was in Europe and his unwillingness to compromise when he returned to the United States.   II

Recognize the purposes for organizing the League of Nations and the United Nations and recognize reasons for the successes and/or failures of each in accomplishing these purposes.   II

Identify the powers and major functions of the United Nations.   I

List three instances in which action taken by the United Nations contributed to the maintenance of world peace or international understanding.   I

Based upon the United Nations charter rules for membership, discuss whether Red China is as entitled to United Nations membership as some present members. Use specific examples in your discussion.   III (SS 710)

SECONDARY

Match each of six functions of the United Nations with the branch (General Assembly, Security Council, Trusteeship Council, Secretariat, Economic and Social Council, International Court of Justice) that carries out the function. I

Given specific world problems, identify which of the following specialized United Nations organizations would handle each problem: FAO (Food and Agriculture Organization), WHO (World Health Organization), UNESCO (United Nations Educational, Scientific, and Cultural Organization), UPU (Universal Postal Union), ITU (International Telecommunications Union), World Bank. I

Identify problems which the United Nations' specialized agencies are best equipped to handle. I

From a list of the contributions of the United Nations during the past twenty years, recognize those that are of a major peacekeeping nature. II

Discuss, in separate paragraphs, five instances during which the United Nations made efforts to keep the peace. III

Summarize three problems that weaken the United Nations. II

Using reasons why the United Nations has been more successful than the League of Nations, predict its future success. III

For each of the following treaty organizations, describe the qualifications for membership and the purposes of each association and explain how each has fulfilled or is fulfilling its purpose: NATO, SEATO, CENTO, OAS, and ANZUS. II

Identify reasons for the interdependency of the economies of European nations and prepare to debate the issues which have resulted in the establishment of such organizations as the Common Market and the Outer Seven. III

Predict the future success of the Common Market and the Outer Seven and discuss the possible extension of these organizations into political alliances. III

Describe two examples of a foreign country's exerting influence on an American historical event. II

Given a list of problems, recognize reasons why each is a significant problem in current world affairs. II

Describe four examples from the last five years which illustrate a nation making international morality an extension of national morality in its dealings with another power. II

Recognize the changes and reasons for changes in the degree of United States involvement in Asian and European affairs from 1920 to 1941. II

Given the following hypothetical situation, predict what steps you think the United States would take, using examples from the past and stated American principles toward Latin America: A large guerrilla force has taken over a section of Bolivia and the government army is not strong enough to put down the revolt. it is reported that the guerrilla forces, although basically Bolivian, have received aid and training from Cuban Communists. III

Write a two-page report showing the change of United States policy toward Latin American affairs from 1898 to the present, citing the following items. III
1. Big Stick Policy
2. Good Neighbor Policy
3. O.A.S.
4. Alliance for Progress
5. United States-Cuban relations in the 1960s
6. Dominican Republic intervention (1965)

From the list below, identify three conflicts between Western and non-Western civilizations and identify the approximate era of each conflict. I
1. Battle of Tours
2. Persian Wars
3. Cold War
4. Boer War
5. Punic Wars

Develop at least a two-page outline of an international pilot program to preserve world peace and conserve human and natural resources consistent with the principle of mutual respect between sovereign competing nations. V (SS 712)

SECONDARY

Using a world-affairs simulation model, pretend that you hold an important position in one of the nations of the real or an imaginary world. Participate in the attempts to meet crises and solve problems that face this world.   III (SS 712)

Using a world-affairs simulation model, analyze the major problem facing the country with whose government you would have to work. Determine the "best" course of action and attempt to get your government to accept and act on your plans. Accept all rules, laws, and situations that are a part of the world-affairs simulation in which you are participating.   IV (SS 712)

Discuss the one goal you feel is more important than any other in human affairs. Using a world-affairs simulation model, attempt to get others to accept the same goal. Work within your own government and with other governments in the model. Continue to work until you have succeeded, have tried at least three different ways of winning acceptance for the idea, or no longer have power to continue. Work only according to the rules of the world-affairs simulation in which you are involved.   III (SS 712)

Write a report of your experiences in a world-affairs simulation model. Evaluate the role you played. Tell at least two decisions you made which you consider "important." Tell one thing you learned which surprised you. Evaluate the successes and failures you experienced in the simulation.   VI

SS 610 Develop guidelines for the foreign policy of an imaginary democratic country that provide for an effective leadership for world peace. Use these guidelines to evaluate given examples of United States foreign policy.   VI

Classify examples of United States foreign policy decisions as either presidential responsibilities or congressional responsibilities.   II

Recognize examples of each of the following United States foreign policies: neutrality, overseas expansion, isolationism, international cooperation, international conflict.   II

Match the following four current international organizations to which the United States belongs with the purpose of each organization: North Atlantic Treaty Organization, Southeast Asia Treaty Organization, Organization of American States, and the United Nations.   I

Write a three- to five-page report on the current United States foreign policy toward any country or any area of the world. III (LA 547)

Analyze an editorial or a political speech which discusses foreign relations, determining the author's viewpoints on foreign policy. IV (LA 565)

Write a two-page dialogue of argument between two persons who hold opposing views on one of the following subjects: (1) American involvement in Vietnam, or (2) American assistance to Israel in the Arab-Israeli war. V (LA 670)

Write a 200-word passage in which you state under what conditions, if any, you think war might be justified. V (SS 712)

Having read a short story, a novel, or a play that deals with the subject of war, describe two different attitudes toward war revealed by the thoughts, speech, and/or actions of two characters. II (LA 640)

SS 615 **Show that you can reasonably predict the future of one of the following countries in the power structure of the world's nations: Soviet Union, Red China, any country in Southeast Asia. III**

Locate and label on an outline map these major industrial regions of the U.S.S.R.: Donnetsky (Donbas, Donetz), Kuznetsky (Kuzbas, Kuznetz), Trans-Volga, South Ural, Leningrad, Central (Moscow), Baku (Caspian), and Eastern Siberia (Irkutsk). I (SS 725)

Discuss the advances which Russia has made in trying to gain each of the following: a warm-water port, additional fur-trapping grounds, greater mineral deposits. III

Make predictions about the influence that the migrations of people to Siberia will have on Soviet economy. III

Discuss the geographic limitations on the U.S.S.R.'s agricultural capability, using data on climatic and physical characteristics and locating each geographic area discussed. III (SS 725)

SECONDARY

Explain four ways that China's experiences with Western powers during the 19th and early 20th centuries led to the development of Chinese hostility and suspicion toward the West today.   II

Express four generalizations about ways in which Communist China's foreign policy resembles and differs from the foreign policy of Imperial China. Explain these generalizations.   II

Form five generalizations about Communist China's foreign policy. Support these generalizations with factual evidence.   IV

Prepare a paper based on library research to show the relationship between limited good land and China's development. Present the paper to a small group for discussion.   III (SS 715)

Develop a hypothetical solution to China's problem of overpopulation. State three reasons why you chose your solution.   V (SS 712)

Explain five reasons for the Sino-Soviet conflict.   II

On an outline map of Southeast Asia, identify the following countries: Burma, Thailand, Cambodia, Laos, North Vietnam, South Vietnam, Malaysia, Indonesia, and the Philippines.   I (SS 725)

Write a paper on, conduct a discussion of, or demonstrate with visual aids, the industrial potential of each country in Southeast Asia. Include a summary of the industrial development of each country at the present time.   III (SS 712)

Support the description of Southeast Asia as an area of strategic world importance using information concerning Southeast Asia's waterways, minerals, location, and political systems.   III

SS 620   Make judgments on the philosophy of Marx as conceived in the U.S.S.R. and in Communist China.   VI

Recognize and describe the major goal of theoretical Marxism.   II

Identify political and economic characteristics common to both Czarist and Communist Russian regimes and characteristics in which the two regimes differ.   I

Recognize from a list the ways in which Lenin revised Marxist ideology to ensure the success of the Communist Revolution in Russia following the collapse of the Czarist regime in March 1917, and explain why he felt these revisions were necessary.   II

Explain four major reasons why Lenin's Bolsheviks came to power in 1917.   II

List at least four methods that the Soviet system used and uses to deal with problems of political dissent and select two examples that illustrate each of these methods.   I

Identify the legal means that Soviet citizens have for initiating a change of laws that they consider contrary to the public interest.   I

Identify the major changes that have taken place in the implementation of Soviet central planning since Joseph Stalin's era.   I

Identify at least three ways in which Soviet economic policies have deviated from Marxist policies and give the major reasons for these deviations.   I

Explain to another student whether or not you think Vladimir Lenin and his successors have succeeded in molding Russian citizens into "new socialist men".   II

Identify political and/or economic characteristics common to both the Imperial and Communist Chinese regimes and characteristics that are unique to each regime.   I

Explain ways in which Mao Tse-tung revised the theories of Marx to seize and retain power in China.   II

Explain five major reasons why Mao Tse-tung's Communists came to power on the Chinese mainland.   II

Describe at least four means which the Chinese Communists have used to enforce conformity to the teachings of Mao Tse-tung and to deal with political dissent at home. Give two examples illustrating each of these means and recognize their effectiveness in compelling conformity to Maoist teachings.   II

Draw your own conclusions on the political rights enjoyed by citizens of the People's Republic of China.   VI

SOCIAL STUDIES

SECONDARY

SS 625 **Make judgments on totalitarianism on the basis of effectiveness, efficiency, and freedom of individuals to make choices. VI**

On a time line with 100-year intervals, identify the beginning and end of the Tudor, Stuart, Bourbon, Romanov, and Hapsburg dynasties. I

Match the names of two Tudor, two Stuart, and two Bourbon monarchs with a policy or practice typical of the monarch. I

Match the "benevolent despots" Peter the Great, Catherine the Great, Maria Theresa, and Frederick the Great with the appropriate country and with one policy each introduced. I

Identify three characteristics of limited monarchy that are not characteristics of an absolute monarchy. I

Write a three- to five-paragraph biography of Charles V, Emperor of the Holy Roman Empire (1519–1556), in which you state at least three reasons for considering him one of the outstanding characters of history. III (SS 715)

Support or refute stated conclusions about the characteristics that differentiate a totalitarian society of the 20th century from a democratic society of the 20th century. III

Use examples from two of the following historical situations to form at least three generalizations about the common political, economic, and psychological conditions that seem to lead to totalitarianism. Then apply the generalizations to a given country to determine whether it is presently totalitarian or is moving toward totalitarianism. IV (SS 712)
1. Germany (1919–1932)
2. Russia (1914–1924)
3. China (1930s and 1940s)

Classify the following political characteristics as similar or different in the following situations: Germany under Hitler, Italy under Mussolini, the Soviet Union under Stalin. II
1. Secret police
2. Academic freedom
3. Free elections
4. Private property rights
5. Protection of people's rights
6. Role of the executive

List one leader of Soviet Russia, one leader of Fascist Italy, and one leader of Nazi Germany and name a policy that each followed or instituted.   I

Write at least three paragraphs comparing 19th- or 20th-century Czarist Russia with the U.S.S.R. today in respect to one social, one political, and one economic characteristic.   III

Match each of the following 20th-century dictators with the country he has governed.   I

Dictators	Countries
Castro	North Vietnam
Franco	China
Hirohito	Spain
Ho Chi Minh	Cuba
Mao Tse-tung	East Germany
Tito	Japan
Trujillo	Yugoslavia
Ulbricht	Dominican Republic

Apply information about the good results and bad results of colonial rule in a Southeast Asian country to support your predictions for the immediate future of democratic rule in a Southeast Asian country.   III (SS 712)

From articles, essays, and poems, make inferences about meanings that are given to human freedom by the author.   IV (LA 565)

GeOGraPHY

**SS 630   Show that you can locate political features on maps and globes.
III (SS 725)**

On an outline map of Latin America locate and label the countries from memory.   I

On an outline map locate the following major countries of south Africa: Senegal, Guinea, Liberia, Ghana, Nigeria, Congo (capital—Kinshasa, formerly Leopoldville), Angola, Republic of South Africa, Rhodesia, Zambia, Mozambique, Tanzania (Tansania), Kenya, Uganda, Ethiopia, and Sudan.   I

SECONDARY

On an outline map of the U.S.S.R. locate and label the countries and water bodies that surround the Soviet Union. I

On an outline map of the U.S.S.R. locate and label the major Soviet Socialist Republics: Estonian S.S.R., Latvian S.S.R., Lithuanian S.S.R., Ukrainian S.S.R., Georgian S.S.R., Moldavian S.S.R., Armenian S.S.R., Kazakh S.S.R., Uzbek S.S.R., and Russian Soviet Federated Socialist Republic. I

On an outline map of Australia locate from memory the boundaries of these six states and one territory: New South Wales, Victoria, Tasmania, Queensland, South Australia, Western Australia, and Northern Territory. I

On an outline map of Southeast Asia locate the following countries: Burma, Thailand, Cambodia, Laos, North Vietnam, South Vietnam, Malaysia, Indonesia, and the Philippines. I

On a political outline map label sixteen countries that are completely in Europe, two that are partly in Asia and partly in Europe, one that is European but not on the continent, and one that is politically divided into communist and noncommunist sectors. I

Using three political maps of Europe, each published twenty-five years apart, briefly explain the changes in the political boundaries of European nations. II

SS 635 Show that you can locate physical features on maps and globes. III (SS 725)

Identify by verbal description or by picture the following major landforms: plain, plateau, mountain, hill. I (SC 805)

Identify by verbal description or by picture these major mountain-building processes: folding, faulting, and volcanism. I (SC 805)

Classify pictures as representative of either a natural physical environment or of a man-made physical environment. II

On a physical outline map of South America locate and label from memory each of the following topographic regions: Guiana Highlands, Llanos, Amazonia, Mato Grosso, Gran Chaco, Pampas, and Patagonia. I

SOCIAL STUDIES

SECONDARY

Locate the following river systems of South America: Orinoco, Parana-La Plate, and Magdalena-Cauca. Explain in writing the importance of each. II

Locate the following topographic regions of Central America: tierra caliente, tierra templada, and tierra fria. Explain in writing the importance of each. II

Given an outline map of Africa, locate and label the following physical features: Sahara Desert, Kalahari Desert, Drakensberg Mountains, Ethiopian Highlands, Ahaggar Mountains, Tibesti Mountains, Atlas Mountains, Atlantic Ocean, Mediterranean Sea, Indian Ocean, Red Sea, Lake Tanganyika, Lake Nyasa, Gulf of Guinea, Gulf of Aden, Lake Victoria, Mozambique Channel, Congo River system, Nile River system, Niger and Benue River systems, Volta River system, Senegal River, Cape of Good Hope, and the Equator. I

From a list of physical features of Africa recognize those that hindered exploration of the interior of the continent. II

Locate the following geographic features on a map and tell whether they are in North Africa or the Middle East: Atlas Mountains, Suez Canal, Jordan River, Sahara Desert, Nile River, Gulf of Aqaba, Tigris and Euphrates Rivers, Zagros Mountains, and Plateau of Anatolia. I

Given a cross-sectional illustration of Africa, match the cross-section with each of these latitudes or longitudes: 0° Lat., 30° S. Lat., 25° E. Long., and 0° Long. I

On an outline map of the U.S.S.R. locate and label the major rivers: Dneiper, Volga, Don, Ural, Pechora, Ob, Irtysh, Yenisey, Lena, and Amur. I

Describe the plains landform in the U.S.S.R. II (SC 800)

Using an atlas, locate and label on an outline map of China and the outlying regions the following physical regions and cities: Manchuria, Inner Mongolia, Sinkiang, the Tibetan Plateau, Red China, Mukden, Peking, Wuhan, Shanghai, Canton, Hong Kong, and Formosa (Taiwan). I

116

SECONDARY

Using an atlas and an outline map of China, locate and label the major lowland regions and the main rivers crossing them: Manchurian Plain, North China Plain (Yellow Plain, Delta of the Hwang Ho), Yangtze Plain, Red Basin (Szechuan Basin), Canton Delta (Si Kiang Delta), Loess Plateau, Hwang Ho (Yellow) River, Hsun Chaing (Si Kiang) River, Yangtze River, Sungari (Sung Hua) River, and Liao (Liao Ho) River. I

Write one to three paragraphs which support or refute the generalization, "Europe is a peninsula of peninsulas" on the Eurasian continent. III (SS 712)

On east-west profiles of Europe at 43°, 46°, and 50° North Latitude, locate the Alps, Apennines, Carpathian, Pyrennees, and Ural mountains. I

On an outline map of Europe locate and label the routes of at least ten major rivers. I

On an outline map of Europe locate and label at least five major seaports. I

On an outline map locate European areas you would classify as Western, Eastern, Southern, Northeastern, Northwestern, Southeastern, and Southwestern. I

On an outline map of Australia locate the three major physical regions of Australia: Western Plateau, Central Basins, and Eastern Highlands. I

SS 640 Show that you can locate climatic regions on maps and globes. III

On an outline map of Africa that identifies air circulation patterns, predict local climatic characteristics of the following patterns: January winds, July winds, and ocean currents. III (SC 810)

On an outline map of Africa locate the following climatic regions: Mediterranean, semiarid (steppe), arid (desert), tropical wet and dry (savanna), tropical wet (rain forest), and humid subtropical. I (SC 815)

On an outline map of the U.S.S.R. locate by general area and label these climatic regions: taiga, tundra, humid continental, Mediterranean, desert, steppe, and vertical (mountain) climates. I (SC 815)

SS 645 **Show that you can locate on maps and globes areas where natural and industrial goods are produced. III (SS 725)**

On an outline map of Africa locate areas where each of the following products are produced in the greatest quantity: rubber, palm oil, peanuts (groundnuts), wheat, high-grade beef cattle, native cattle, tobacco, sugar, grapes, citrus fruits, bananas, and cacao (cocoa). I

From a list of minerals (copper, gold, diamonds, cobalt, uranium, bauxite, tin, petroleum) used in United States industry, locate one region in Africa that produces each. I

Locate and label on an outline map these major industrial regions of U.S.S.R.: Donnetsky (Donbas, Donetz), Kuznetsky (Kuzbas, Kuznetz), Trans-Volga, South Ural, Leningrad, Central (Moscow), Baku (Caspian), and Eastern Siberia (Irkutsk). I

On an outline map of Europe identify with symbols sources or locations of fuel, metal, and limestone. With other symbols identify five or more major industrial locations. I

SS 650 **Show that you can use political, physical, and climatic features of a given location to make reasonable predictions on one of the following: (1) agricultural production, (2) economic development, (3) cultural identities of the population. III**

Classify ten resources of Egypt, Morocco, and Israel as either developed or underdeveloped. Suggest uses for the underdeveloped resources. II

Write a paper or give an oral presentation relating amount of rainfall to these types of African occupations: plantation farming, subsistence farming, nomadic herding, and hunting and gathering. III (SC 815, LA 712)

Based on the climatic characteristics needed for producing the world's major cereal food crops, predict the harvest of these crops: rye, barley, rice, corn, and wheat. Use an outline climatic map of the world to locate the main areas where each of these crops is produced.   III (SC 825)

Recognize three climate-changing effects of the deforestation and overgrazing which have occurred in the Middle East and North Africa.   II (SC 590)

Recognize two major differences in the economies of cultures in tropical and temperate climates.   II (SS 530)

Using a population distribution map of Australia, locate the areas where most of the people live and tell why they live there.   II (SC 825)

Identify three geographic characteristics of Middle Eastern and North African population centers which have more than one million people.   I

From maps, charts, and graphs showing birth rate, death rate, life expectancy, and population shifts in our country, recognize the generalizations that describe the graphic data most accurately.   II (SS 710)

In three to five paragraphs support or refute the idea that "cities and urbanization result from cultural, not geographical, causes".   III

Discuss local reasons for not using one of these products as food: beef cattle, hogs, sheep, and turkeys.   III

On a world outline map locate areas of production and human consumption of one grain, one meat, one vegetable, or one fruit. (Choose from the following: oats, rice, or wheat; beef, fish, mutton, or pork; carrots, potatoes, or tomatoes; apples, oranges, or pineapples.)   I

Discuss at least three ways in which geography and ecology have affected culture.   III

Describe cultural practices of three countries, some of which are determined by geography, some of which are not.   II

Recognize two examples that indicate a culture has retained practices probably originated under different geographical conditions.   II

For each of the following groups of people, identify at least two countries where that particular group forms the majority of the population: Europeans, Indians, Mestizos, and Negroes. I

Identify the three major Indian nations found in Latin America in pre-Columbian times and locate the area where each lived. I

From a list of geographic statements about Red China, suggest where you would expect to find a concentration of most of China's population. II

Prepare a paper based on library research showing the relationship between limited arable land and China's development. Present the paper to a small group for discussion. III (LA 525)

For each of the following national groups within the U.S.S.R., locate the region in which they live and tell the approximate number of people in each group: Finns, Ukrainians, Armenians, Uzbekians, Latvians, Lithuanians, Estonians, Byelorussians, and Georgians. I

Looking at a population distribution map of the U.S.S.R., recognize relationships between population centers and physical factors, climatic conditions, and political factors. II

Recognize from a list of statements about the U.S.S.R. those that are a result of historical development and those that are a result of the physical environment. II

Discuss the geographic limitations of the U.S.S.R.'s agricultural capability using data on climatic and physical characteristics. Locate each area discussed. III

Identify three geographic conditions necessary in a grape- and wine-producing region and locate one European area that provides all three conditions. I

Describe at least five geographically based similarities and differences in the economies of one of the following pairs of countries: England and Spain, Italy and Poland, Greece and France, Austria and Norway, Portugal and Switzerland, or France and Germany. II

SECONDARY

Prepare and present an oral report on three relationships between industrialization, population, and transportation in Europe. III (LA 515)

Research and write a three- to five-page plan stressing geographic development in a country or region you have chosen to study. V (SS 710)

Review methods for dealing with problems caused by man's changing his environment. Include the following. V (SC 590)
1. A description of the problem
2. Information that pertains to the problem
3. Causes and effects of the problem
4. Comparison of possible solutions
5. The desired outcome
6. Evaluation of the best possible solution
7. Criteria for judging how well the plan works

economics

SS 655 Make judgments on steps for prevention or correction of a depression advocated by different political groups on the basis of their effect on (1) the economic health of the nation, and (2) the welfare of individuals. VI

Describe the characteristics of a depression, its effects on society, and the steps government can take in preventing a depression. II

Describe documented situations that illustrate five ways in which the private business sector is aided by government (local, state, or federal) in the United States. II

Describe documented situations that illustrate five ways in which the private business sector is limited by government (local, state, or federal) in the United States. II

Recognize three economic problems that contributed to the Depression of 1929. II

Describe the legislative measures sponsored by the Roosevelt Administration that gave new power to labor in its relations with management and in the economy generally. II

Explain legislative measures sponsored by the Roosevelt Administration which dealt with the problems that faced agriculture in the 1930s, and describe how these legislative measures were intended to alleviate the problems of the farmer. II

Support or refute this statement with documented evidence: "The second New Deal (1935–38) was much more responsive to the nonbusiness segment of the economy than the first New Deal (1932–34)." III (SS 710)

Using criteria such as unemployment levels, gross national product, banking assets, industrial investment, and other related analyses, support this statement: "By 1939, the New Deal had generally failed to solve the major problems of the Depression." III (LA 547)

Evaluate the arguments used in three current economic controversies in the United States and decide which position you support on each issue. VI (SS 720)

SS 660   Make judgments on three current proposals for solving problems of poverty in the United States.   VI

Recognize causes of poverty in America and groups of people that are poverty-stricken in America today. II

Discuss causes of slums and ghettos. Support, with factual evidence, one of the solutions offered by sociologists or politicians for problems of slums and ghettos. III

Recognize problems associated with slum clearance projects and urban redevelopment. II

Develop a plan for a slum clearance project that resolves the major difficulties associated with such projects. V (SS 712)

Explain how industrialization causes urbanization and how increased urbanization stimulates the growth of industry. II

Present a panel discussion on elimination of jobs by technology. Consider what is being done, or should be done, to create new jobs. (You should have documented information to use in your discussion.) IV (LA 525)

SECONDARY

Write a two- or three-page report discussing the resources of an underdeveloped region of the United States. III (SS 710)

Answer the following questions about the Social Security Act. I
1. When was the Act passed?
2. Who is eligible?
3. Who pays for the program?
4. What benefits are paid?
5. Who administers the program?
6. How has the Social Security Act been amended?

Write a paper or give an oral report in which you discuss each of five social-welfare problems in the United States and the social programs suggested or used to help solve each problem. III (SS 710)

Discuss the proposals of economists and politicians that insure a base income for every household in the United States. III

Develop a five-year program whereby a 16-year-old boy or girl living in an underprivileged area can find ample opportunity to acquire the skills necessary to live a productive life in the United States. Before you put your program in final form, clearly define the terms *underprivileged area* and *productive life* and do the research necessary for the development of such a program. V

Discuss major features of the current Poverty Program and predict its successes or failures based on evidence gathered from your research. III

Develop your own solution to the problem of poverty and welfare in America. V (SS 720)

SS 665   Show that you can discuss the economic problems and potentials of any area of your choice and can suggest a solution for each problem. V (SS 712)

Using the following terms, discuss how production is increased in an economic system: (1) capital, (2) labor, (3) natural resources, (4) technology. III

From a list of statements of Latin American economic problems, recognize statements that can be directly traced to Latin America's colonial heritage. II

On the basis of what you have learned about the economies of the subregions of Latin America, develop guidelines for economists who want to solve the economic problems of each region. V

Discuss the advances Russia has made in trying to gain each of the following: a warm-water port, additional fur-trapping grounds, greater mineral deposits. III

Summarize information that explains the recent migration of Russians to Siberia. II

Tell how the economy of China compares with the economy of the Soviet Union. II

Evaluate listed statements concerning the Communists' efforts to improve China's economy in respect to their success. VI

Develop a hypothetical solution to China's problem of overpopulation. State three reasons why you chose your solution. V (SS 712)

Write a research paper containing information that supports the hypothesis that China may pose a threat to the West in the next twenty years. III (SS 715)

Write a paper on, conduct a discussion of, or demonstrate with visual aids the industrial potential of each country in Southeast Asia. Include a summary of the industrial development of each country at the present time. III (SS 712)

Use information concerning Southeast Asia's waterways, minerals, location, and political systems to support the description of Southeast Asia as an area of strategic world importance. III

From a list of statements about Australia's imports, exports, production, pastoral industries, agriculture, mineral resources, and size, identify the statements that are true. I

SECONDARY

Explain the flow of exports and imports for both Australia and New Zealand. II

From a list of statements on New Zealand's standard of living, imports, exports, pastoral industries, dairy products, water resources, and production, identify the statements that are true. I

Identify statements that summarize how two countries of Europe have used trade to maintain their economies and living standards. I

Classify the resources of Egypt, Morocco, and Israel as either developed or underdeveloped. Suggest uses for the underdeveloped resources. II

Present evidence to support or refute the statement that "we owe the national debt to ourselves." III

Explain five reasons for the rising national debt in the United States. II

Present evidence to support or refute the argument that "the national debt will lead to bankruptcy and will saddle the next generation with the burden of paying off the national debt." III (LA 547, SS 705)

Present evidence for and against balancing the national budget as a means of coping with an inflationary trend and preserving domestic tranquility. III (LA 547, SS 705)

Define the term *inflation* and tell the effects of inflation on a society. I

Evaluate measures the United States government has taken to slow down or stop inflation during two different inflationary periods. IV

Given a list of occupational groups in society, recognize those that are hurt most by inflation, and explain why these groups are hurt most. II

SS 670   Show that you can discuss the advantages and disadvantages of a completely free enterprise system, a controlled economy, and a mixed economy.   III

> Identify accurate descriptions of each of the following types of economies: capitalistic, communistic, socialistic, and mixed-market economies.   I
>
> Classify three criticisms raised by 19th-century social novelists under one or more of the following categories: economic, political, or social criticism.   II (LA 660)
>
> Summarize the major social contributions of each of the following men: Charles Fourier, Robert Owen, and Claude Saint-Simon.   II
>
> Write three paragraphs about capitalism. In each paragraph, describe a practice of capitalism that Marx criticized and that was modified by the capitalistic system.   III (LA 545)
>
> Write a paper or give a talk outlining three effects of the industrial revolution in Europe on Asia, Africa, and South America.   III (LA 545)
>
> Identify correct definitions for the following economic terms: (1) economics, (2) goods and services, (3) value, (4) production, (5) resources, (6) consumption, (7) income, (8) capital, (9) supply, (10) demand, (11) public, (12) private, (13) profit, (14) competition, (15) incentive, (16) free enterprise, and (17) market.   I
>
> Identify economic needs and characteristics common to all societies.   I
>
> Given descriptions of economic systems, identify those systems that are explanations of (1) American capitalism, (2) British socialism, and (3) Russian communism.   I
>
> Classify statements on prices, wages, government regulation of the economy, economic competition, labor unions, production, and individual welfare as capitalistic, socialistic, or communistic.   II
>
> Name the major sources of union and business power and the methods used by each source to retain or increase its power or to limit the power of other sources.   I

SECONDARY

Recognize two major changes in the labor movement over the last several decades. Predict changes that may develop in the next several decades. III

Given an example of a labor-management dispute, suggest means of resolving the dispute. II

Define a social problem created by the conflict between labor and business and evaluate possible ways to solve the problem. VI (SS 712)

Discuss the advantages and disadvantages to society that result from strong labor unions. III

Given an allocation problem, determine what would be relinquished by using the scarce resource in alternate ways. Select the alternative that seems to involve the least cost. IV

Describe how decisions about the following questions are made in a traditional society. II
1. What kinds of goods and services will be produced?
2. How will goods and services be produced?
3. For whom will goods and services be produced?

Describe how decisions about the following questions are made in a command economic system. II
1. What kinds of goods and services will be produced?
2. How will goods and services be produced?
3. For whom will goods and services be produced?

Draw three circular flow diagrams and illustrate how and where you and your family's specific economic roles fit into the following circular flows of goods and services. III
1. Between the public and producers
2. Between the public and the government
3. Between savers and investors

Given a list of statements, identify those that describe how prices are determined in model competitive product markets and factor markets. I

Given a situation in which the price of a product or a service changes, predict probable consequences to production and consumption of the product or service. III

Recognize examples of the following characteristics of monopolies and oligopolies in the modified market system in the United States. II
1. The main ways they hinder the operation of a perfect market model
2. The main reasons why monopolies and oligopolies developed and why they still exist
3. The most effective restraints that are placed on monopolies and oligopolies so that a modified market system is retained

Write an essay that supports or refutes regulation of the United States economy, based on your understanding of capitalism as in contemporary America, socialism in England, and communism in the U.S.S.R.   IV

SS 675   Make judgments on taxes your parents pay in relation to these factors.   VI
1. The equity of tax payments in relation to ability to pay
2. The equity of tax in relation to equal responsibility in a democracy
3. The services provided by taxes through local, state, and federal government action

Present evidence to support or refute the idea that the progressive income tax as applied to private citizens and private corporations is based on ability to pay.   III

Recognize two possible effects of each of the following situations upon the nation's economy.   II
1. Increased taxes matched by increased government spending during wartime
2. Increased taxes matched by reduced government spending during peacetime
3. Reduced taxes matched by an increase in government spending during peacetime
4. Leaving taxes unchanged but increasing government spending during peacetime

Explain why the oil depletion allowance, the loss-offset system, and agricultural support prices represent inequities in the United States tax structure.   II

SECONDARY

Give at least five examples to explain how the interpretation of the federal government's power to tax has changed since the United States Constitution was written. II

Write several paragraphs using at least five specific facts from United States history or from current United States affairs that support or negate the position that taxes are necessary to support a civilized society. III (LA 547, SS 710)

SS 680 Show that you can find solutions to personal economic problems. III

Identify two ways to buy a product for less than its customary price. I

Suggest two advantages and two disadvantages of credit buying. II

Identify an advantage of each type of insurance: term, endowment, straight life. I

Identify advantages and costs of health-insurance programs. I

Describe purposes and means of saving and investing. II

Given a person's annual salary, exemptions, deductions, and amount of withheld tax and using tax reference materials, complete a federal income tax form. III

Develop a hypothetical investment portfolio in which you invest a given sum of money in at least two different companies, and write a two-page statement explaining your investment pattern. Include in your statement the following information. V
1. Why you would like to make an investment
2. Investment possibilities that you have considered and the opportunity and costs involved in these alternatives
3. A brief description of the companies in which you are investing
4. How and why your investment plans will meet your investment objectives

PSYCHOLOGY aND PHILOSOPHY

SS 685 Show your understanding of aspects of careers in the following occupational areas: building trades, business, technical services, and social services.   II (SS 720)

Identify the main duties of carpenters, painters, plumbers, bricklayers, construction-machinery operators, and construction electricians.   I

Identify the employment opportunities and the usual training methods in the building trades.   I

Identify various jobs in the family of building-trade occupations.   I

Identify the work activities of typists, stenographers, secretaries, and file clerks.   I

Identify the employment opportunities for clerical workers.   I

Identify the amount and type of education and the basic skills usually required for typists, stenographers, and secretaries.   I

Identify three occupations in the field of biological science.   I

Identify employment opportunities for engineers.   I

Tell what type of courses and how much education are required for engineers.   I

Identify typical work activities of the following types of engineers: electrical, civil, mechanical, and aerospace.   I

Describe the difference between the work done by engineering and physical-science technicians, and the work done by engineers and scientists.   II

Identify the major duties of draftsmen.   I

SECONDARY

Identify the main work activities and employment opportunities of computer programmers.   I

Identify typical work activities of photographers.   I

Identify typical work activities of architects.   I

Identify the employment opportunities in your own area for one of the technical occupations.   I

Identify typical work activities and the amount and type of education required for bookkeepers.   I

Identify typical work activities of bank tellers.   I

Identify typical educational requirements and employment opportunities for office machine operators.   I

Identify various jobs that are included in the family of business occupations.   I

Identify the main work tasks of the following health service technicians: medical technologist, medical X-ray technician, dental hygienist, and dental-laboratory technician.   I

List three major areas in which life-science technicians specialize.   I

Recognize, from a list, the topics that would most likely be the concern of botanists, microbiologists, or zoologists.   II

Identify the employment opportunities and educational requirements for biological scientists.   I

Identify various jobs that are included in the family of technical occupations.   I

Identify how much and what kind of education is generally required for technical occupations.   I

Identify the field of study for the following social sciences: anthropology, economics, geography, history, political science, psychology, and sociology.   I

Match work activities to the appropriate social scientist: anthropologist, economist, geographer, historian, political scientist, psychologist, or sociologist. I

Identify typical work activities of social workers. I

Identify employment opportunities and the amount and kind of education usually required for social workers. I

Identify the main work activities and the amount of education required for clergymen, priests, and rabbis. I

Identify the type and amount of education required to become a lawyer and the major types of problems with which lawyers typically assist clients. I

Identify the ways to prepare for careers in acting or dancing and the employment opportunities for actors, actresses, and dancers. I

Describe the employment opportunities for music teachers and performers. II

Identify the major ways that one can prepare for a career as a singer or singing teacher. I

SS 690   Make judgments on two possible career choices for yourself. Use these criteria: (1) interest, (2) developed abilities scores, (3) performance in related objectives, (4) job potential, (5) salary potential and fringe benefits, (6) congruency with your value system.   VI (SS 720)

Identify five kinds of information used in comparing jobs: (1) duties of the job, (2) entry requirements, (3) working conditions, (4) amount and kind of benefits received, (5) opportunities for employment on the job. I

Given a job catalogue, find answers to specific questions about a particular job. II

Classify jobs according to elements they have in common. II

SECONDARY

Interview at least two people working in the occupations you have chosen and obtain information regarding (1) the job, (2) entry requirements, (3) working conditions, (4) amount and kind of benefits received, (5) opportunities for employment on the job. II

Identify five factors that people consider in choosing a job. I

Describe jobs that would probably be satisfying to a person, based on a description of what that person desires in a job. II

Identify two things a high school student can do to prepare for future career decisions. I

Evaluate your grades, test scores, and other related information in relation to possible occupation choices. V

Compare and contrast potential occupational choices in respect to your value system. V

SS 695 **Using your own set of social values as a basis for analysis, demonstrate your ability to perceive the difficulties individuals meet in living according to their values under the social controls imposed by their own community. Consider these problems: (1) the compromises an individual should or should not make in living in that community; (2) the impact the implementation of an individual's social values might have on his community; (3) the psychological problems for an individual who is forced to compromise his values.   IV**

After reading definitions of the following terms that are associated with the concept of social control, rewrite them in your own words to show you understand their meanings: (1) laws, (2) norms, (3) conformity, (4) social role, (5) social expectation, (6) social institution, (7) stability, (8) peer group, (9) social structure, (10) socially deviant behavior, (11) social dissent, (12) folkways, and (13) mores. II

Given case studies, readings, or other statements on social control, classify statements into the categories of (1) laws, (2) mores, and (3) folkways. II

Discuss the controls exercised by the following institutions. Consider the changes in controls during the last twenty-five years and predict future changes in these controls: (1) family, (2) government, (3) economics, (4) education, (5) religion, or (6) shared by more than one institution.   III

Given the following examples involving conflict between mores and laws, recognize reasons for the conflict: (1) the 18th Amendment, (2) women's rights, and (3) religion and education.   II (SS 545)

Given situations of human group behavior, describe examples of the following characteristics of groups: (1) the goals of the group (immediate and/or long range); (2) the patterns of roles and status in the group; and (3) the norms or the generally accepted standard of behavior recognized by group members.   II

Given situations of human group behavior in which one or more of the following types of conflicts occur, predict the probable consequences of the conflict; propose alternate solutions to remove the conflict; and, after evaluating the plans, decide which one would provide the most appropriate solution: (1) conflicts about group goals, (2) conflicts about role behavior (differences in role expectations), and (3) conflicts about group norms.   VI

Determine the probable source of power in situations where a group or an individual has power over another group or individual.   IV

Develop a theory that relates the universal needs of men to the development of basic elementary political systems and basic elementary economic systems to meet those needs.   V (SS 712)

Write and present a brief skit that identifies a group of people joined to achieve a particular purpose. One member of the group should obviously contribute to, or detract from, the achievement of the group.   III (LA 525)

Describe how the following agents socialize political attitudes and behaviors and explain what political attitudes and/or behaviors you have learned from these agents: (1) family unit, (2) formal educational institutions, (3) peer groups, (4) employment situations, (5) mass media, and (6) direct contacts with the political system.   II

SECONDARY

Analyze the following statement on the basis of social, legal, and economic conditions which have characterized the status of the Negro in the United States: "The Negro in America has been subject to a system designed to destroy his ambition, to prevent his independence, and to make him wonder if he really does exist." IV (SS 500)

From a list of stated conflicts, suggest the reason for the Supreme Court's desegregation decision in the case of *Brown* v. *Board of Education* (1954) and the political-moral conflict that has arisen from this decision. II (SS 500)

For each of the areas listed, suggest one example of a development (since 1946) which led to a rise in the status of Negroes as a group: (1) athletics, (2) government, (3) education, (4) entertainment, (5) ethnic identification, (6) business, and (7) political awareness. II (SS 500)

Given statements advocating integration, separatism, and segregation of the black man in America, support one position. In defending your position, state why you chose it over the other two statements. III (SS 500)

Given four specific values held by the majority of Americans, analyze the motives behind statements made by members of the majority groups about behaviors of minority groups. IV (SS 705)

Given a selection from a list of literary works dealing with social injustice, recognize attitudes held by characters in the works that either cause or reinforce unjust social conditions. II (LA 660)

Briefly describe two actions for each of the following types of characters from short stories, novels, and plays you have read: a character whose actions are entirely responsible, a character whose actions are responsible in some respects, a character whose actions are entirely irresponsible. Select actions that have important consequences for the character who performs them and for others. Explain why your examples are valid. III (LA 640)

Based on your observations of conformity in novels, short stories, plays, and life, write an extended definition of the term *conformity*. III (LA 660)

Given novels, short stories, and plays that you have read, recognize the areas in which the major character in each conformed with the social standards of society at the time depicted, and the areas in which he did not.   II (LA 645)

Describe the consequences of the unconventionality of a given literary character who is a nonconformist.   II (LA 645)

Given characters in novels and plays about human society that you have read, analyze their general behavior as consistent or inconsistent with the following definition of *civilized behavior*: "Civilized behavior is the extent of concern one's actions show for the welfare of other people." In a sentence or two, explain your analysis of the behavior of each character.   IV (LA 645)

Given a literary work that deals with people in a particular society, recognize in the makings of that society examples of the following elements: (1) political, (2) economic, (3) educational, (4) leisure time, or avocational, (5) social, and (6) spiritual, or religious. For example, a competitive grading system is an educational element in our civilization; the stock market and the graduated income tax are economic elements.   II (LA 660)

Having recognized elements in the makeup of a particular society described in novels and plays that you have read, analyze these as elements that encourage civilized behavior, elements that encourage and discourage civilized behavior, or elements that discourage civilized behavior. As a guide to analyzing the different elements, use the following definition of *civilized behavior*: "Civilized behavior is the extent of concern a person's actions show for the welfare of other people."   IV (LA 660)

Identify three privileges or immunities provided by the 14th Amendment that protect United States citizens against unfair actions by their state governments.   I (SS 570)

SS 700   Demonstrate your ability to combine concepts, principles, and generalizations by developing a list of criteria for selection of a religion most suitable for the individual.   V

Recognize five beliefs of the Judeo-Christian tradition and suggest how they may have affected our contemporary social environment both positively and negatively.   II

SECONDARY

Present evidence (pictures, objects, copies) of nine different artifacts (three documents, three architectural forms, and three art objects) that are representative of the Judeo-Christian tradition. III

Represent on a time line the chronological order of major military events in the Judeo-Christian tradition. II

Discuss the meaning of the term *individualism* as it relates to the Judeo-Christian system of ethics. III

Identify heroes and martyrs who are prominent in Judeo-Christian history. I

Make an outline map of the world to represent the expansion of Judeo-Christian culture for each of these dates: A.D. 100, A.D. 1000, A.D. 1400, and A.D. 1900. III (SS 725)

Recognize the similarities of Mohammedanism, Hinduism, Confucianism, Judaism, and Christianity. II

Discuss characteristics of three religions that interest you. III

Review the contemporary religious trends of American society, relating concern with religion to an awareness of social problems. Use your information to predict the form and direction religion will take in the next century. III (SS 712)

SOCIAL STUDIES INQUIRY SKILLS

SS 705   Demonstrate your ability to perceive the relevance of social science data to the topic being considered, the authority of its source, and its freedom from bias.   IV

Given the name of a historian and a quotation from his writing, classify his frame of reference as economic, geographic, political, or religious. II

Determine whether interpretations of each of the following histori-cal developments are logical or nonlogical: the rise of Egyptian civilization, the rise of China's Yellow River civilization, and the rise of Indus River civilization.   IV (SS 505)

Analyze a one-page written document, drawing inferences about the probable point of view of the author, the intended audience, and the purpose of the document.   IV (LA 565)

Analyze given statements to determine whether they are judg-ments of fact, inferences, or value judgments.   IV (LA 600)

Given a body of data, form generalizations that are supported by the data.   IV

Determine valid deductive arguments (syllogism) and invalid ones. Identify the source of the fallacies.   IV

Analyze examples of the following logical fallacies and rewrite the examples to make them logically correct: (1) undefined or abstract terms, (2) overgeneralization, (3) post hoc, ergo, propter hoc (after this, therefore, because of this), (4) false analogies, (5) non sequitur, (6) ignoratio elenchi (arguing off the point), and (7) sampling (insuf-ficient evidence).   IV

Recognize the irrelevant statements in a given written passage.   II

Recognize the definition of each of the following terms, and recog-nize an example of each term: (1) bias, (2) data, (3) fact, (4) frame of reference, (5) generalization, (6) hypothesis, (7) interpretation, (8) internal criticism, (9) logical fallacy, (10) primary sources, and (11) secondary sources.   II

Differentiate between historical statements that are factual and statements that are interpretive.   II

Given a historical hypothesis and data, differentiate between the data that support the hypothesis and the data that do not support it.   II

SECONDARY

Given conflicting interpretations of a historical event, determine the facts or assumptions that created points of difference between the two interpretations.   IV

Develop a research project on a topic that interests you and that has historical significance in American studies.   V

Given a reading selection containing a theme supported by facts, support the accuracy of the details by consulting appropriate special references.   III

In writing and/or in a discussion, analyze both written and oral presentations to identify information that is relevant or irrelevant to the topic.   IV (LA 547)

In writing and/or in a discussion, analyze both written and oral presentations to identify faulty generalizations.   IV (LA 565)

Analyze a news story as reported in two different publications, broadcasts, or telecasts to identify examples of bias or misleading use of facts revealed in the different ways the two media dealt with the same story.   IV (LA 695)

Given examples of common propaganda devices, classify them as associated with (1) name calling, (2) glittering generalities, (3) transfer, (4) testimonial, (5) plain folks, (6) card stacking, and (7) band wagon.   II

Given examples of common propaganda appeals, classify them as associated with (1) survival, (2) safety, (3) belonging, (4) prestige, and (5) fulfillment.   II

After identifying the primary motive of a particular propagandist, classify the motive into one of the following categories.   II
1. Shows little concern other than for his or his group's welfare
2. Shows about as much concern for others as for his or his group's welfare
3. Shows more concern for others than for his or his group's welfare

Given the name and a brief description of a past propaganda campaign, find additional information about the campaign so that you may complete the following tasks. You must support the validity of the direct consequence you list by identifying the sources of your information. Furthermore, you must list at least two different sources of information.   III (SS 712)
1. Describe one direct consequence of the compaign.
2. Describe two indirect consequences that possibly resulted from the campaign.
3. Form generalizations about propaganda campaigns.

Develop a propaganda campaign for or against an idea or action. Your piece of propaganda must meet the following requirements.   V
1. It must make use of at least one of the common propaganda devices.
2. It must make use of at least one of the common propaganda appeals.

SS 710   Demonstrate your ability to use information sources as required in social studies.   III

Identify the reference book, or books, that could be used to find each of the facts listed below.   I
Reference books
Readers' Guide to Periodical Literature   Almanac
Historical atlas   Dictionary
Atlas   Encyclopedia
1. The author of a magazine article
2. The African colonies in 1914
3. The physical geography of Europe
4. United States population by states, 1790–1960
5. Magazine articles on elections
6. A brief biography of Thomas Jefferson
7. A political map of Europe in 1648
8. A list of presidents of the United States

Classify the following as primary or secondary documents: (1) newspaper articles, (2) textbook describing Napoleon's Battle of Waterloo, (3) novel, (4) critique of a novel, (5) research proposal, and (6) letter to a friend.   II

SECONDARY

SS 712 Demonstrate your ability to present and support a hypothesis pertaining to an area of social studies. Your presentation may be written or oral and may take the form of a plan or a simulation model. **V**

SS 715 Demonstrate your ability to combine concepts, principles, and generalizations by using varied resource materials to develop a library research paper in which you present a hypothesis related to a social studies problem. **V**

> Given the title of a book, use the card catalogue in a library to find: (1) the author of the book, (2) the publisher of the book, (3) the copyright date of the book, (4) the subject of the book, and (5) the call number of the book. II
>
> Find or use the following abbreviations in written research: (1) ibid., (2) loc. cit., (3) op. cit., (4) et al., (5) etc., (6) f. or ff., (7) p. or pp., (8) ed., (9) sic, and (10) vol. or vols. III
>
> Using a model, write a footnote for material found in a book or magazine. III
>
> Demonstrate ability to use the card catalogue, the *Readers' Guide to Periodical Literature,* and any other special indexes in your school or community library. III
>
> Using acceptable form, prepare working bibliography cards in an acceptable style and use the listings to construct a final bibliography. III
>
> Select a topic for research that meets the following criteria. III
> 1. It is of interest to you as a researcher.
> 2. It is researchable from sources available to you.
> 3. It is sufficiently limited to allow scholarly consideration.
>
> Write a research paper that meets all of the established rules on form and style. Your paper will include (1) a title page, (2) an introductory statement that explains and limits the topic, (3) conclusions drawn as a result of the research, (4) footnotes as appropriate, and (5) a complete bibliography. III

SS 720   Demonstrate your ability to make judgments regarding personal decisions based on reliable data.   VI

SS 725   Demonstrate your ability to use maps and globes as needed in social studies.   III

appenDix

TERMINAL OBJECTIVES

HIStory

PRIMARY

SS 005   Show your understanding of changes in communities and reasons for them.   II

INTERMEDIATE

SS 200   Show that you can discuss the reasons that Europeans and, later, people from other parts of the world settled in North America and the problems they encountered.   III

SS 205   Show your understanding of cultural and economic aspects of life in early America.   II

SS 210   On the basis of human goals and needs, make judgments about the events that led to the American Revolution. Consider the issues from the viewpoints of the English and of the American colonists.   VI

SS 215   Show your understanding of the following aspects of your state's history by describing them: culture, natural environment, industrial development, government services, social problems.   II

SS 220   Find information on a topic of your own choice concerning the War Between the States.   II

SS 225   Show your understanding of urban settlement patterns by describing the settlement of two cities in terms of the reasons for the locations.   II

SS 230   Show your understanding of urban growth patterns by describing the growth of two cities in terms of (1) the industries that led to rapid growth, and (2) the unique characteristics of each city.   II

SS 235   Show that you can prepare and present a report showing how urban problems in the last half of the 19th century compare with urban problems of today.   III

TERMINAL OBJECTIVES

SS 240 Show that you can discuss the reasons that Europeans and, later, people from other parts of the world settled in Latin America and the problems they encountered.   III

SECONDARY

SS 500 Demonstrate your ability to combine concepts, principles, and generalizations by developing a hypothesis concerning the history of racial conflict in the United States between the white majority and the black minority.   V

SS 505 Make a judgment on the requirement of study of early civilizations using these criteria: (1) inherent value of acquiring knowledge, (2) relation to understanding of human nature, (3) relation to resolving present-day conflicts, and (4) appreciation of human endeavors.   VI

SS 510 Make judgments on statements that indicate the contributions of medieval, Rennaissance, and non-Western medieval cultures to present society.   VI

SS 515 Make judgments on statements that indicate the contributions the Industrial Revolution has made to 20th-century political movements and economic organizations.   VI

SS 520 Show that you can participate in a debate involving the historical significance of a current issue in your state.   III

SOCIOLOGY and ANTHROPOLOGY

PRIMARY

SS 010 Show your understanding of the interdependence of people in families.   II

SS 015 Show your understanding of types of neighborhoods.   II

SS 020 Show your understanding of types of communities and their characteristic customs.   II

SS 025 Show your understanding of the interdependence of people in communities.   II

SOCIAL STUDIES

TERMINAL OBJECTIVES

SS 030 Show your understanding of the interdependence of communitites.   II

INTERMEDIATE

SS 245 Show your understanding of the changing character of rural life.   II

SS 250 Show that you can discuss the changes that technology has made in human society and can predict changes that technology may bring about in the near future.   III

SS 255 By forming generalizations, demonstrate your ability to perceive changing attitudes toward education and leisure time and the resultant problems in communities.   IV

SS 256 Show that you can reasonably predict the growth and changes of the American family in relation to traditional attitudes toward family functions, social values, and other social institutions.   III

SS 260 Make a judgment about the progress the United States has made in solving the problems of ethnic groups.   VI

SS 265 Show that you can discuss the relationship between ecological problems of the world and the current focus on population control.   III

SS 270 Show that you can support or refute government control of drugs, alcohol, and tobacco.   III

SS 275 Show that you can find a variety of evidence that demonstrates the important traditions and cultural contributions made by Latin Americans and Indians to Western civilization.   III

SS 280 By drawing conclusions from historical and sociological data, show your understanding of reasons for cultural and economic problems existing in Latin America today.   II

SOCIAL STUDIES

TERMINAL OBJECTIVES

SS 285 Demonstrate your ability to combine concepts, principles, and generalizations by developing a plan that you would support for solving a social problem. V

SECONDARY

SS 525 Show that you can support or refute the prediction that a period of racial conflict will precede a period of racial equality and peaceful coexistence. III

SS 530 By forming generalizations, demonstrate your ability to perceive reasons for cultural differences among peoples of the world. IV

SS 535 Demonstrate your ability to combine concepts, principles, and generalizations by proposing solutions to problems created for individuals by advancing technology. V

SS 540 Demonstrate your ability to combine concepts, principles, and generalizations by developing a campaign to educate the members of your community about local ecology problems. Your campaign should include materials for all age groups and work groups. Provide for implementation of resource protection devices. V

SS 545 Demonstrate your ability to combine concepts, principles, and generalizations by writing a paper that explains the need for social change in the area of women's rights. V

SS 550 Given five urban problems, make judgments on suggested solutions. VI

POLITICAL SCIENCE

PRIMARY

SS 035 Show that you know some factors involved in the process of government. I

148

TERMINAL OBJECTIVES

INTERMEDIATE

SS 290   Show your understanding of the effect on the writers of the American Constitution of attempts to organize a government structure in colonial America.   II

SS 295   By analyzing statements on current issues, demonstrate your ability to perceive conflicts among United States political leaders over the purpose and role of government. List current conflicts and conflicts among early American political leaders.   IV

SS 300   Demonstrate your ability to perceive the relationship of civilian control problems to civil rights.   IV

SS 305   Demonstrate your ability to perceive relationships between political problems and legislative action.   IV

SS 310   Show that you can discuss basic needs that should be met by the laws and rules of a society.   III

SS 315   Demonstrate your ability to combine concepts, principles, and generalizations by developing a set of political values based on information you have analyzed.   V

SS 320   Show that you can find and use information from both sides of the issue to write a summary of the advantages and disadvantages of two or more solutions that have been offered for a current conflict between nations.   III

SS 325   Show that you can discuss the political features of a country.   III

SS 330   Show your understanding of the relationship of problems of individuals to their form of government.   II

SECONDARY

SS 555   Show that you can support or refute the following statement: "The United States Constitution was written as a guide for all times. Changing it or interpreting it within the context of new attitudes or beliefs violates the intent of our founding fathers."   III

SOCIAL STUDIES

TERMINAL OBJECTIVES

SS 560   Show your understanding of the forms and functions of our government by matching listed problems to the branch of government most directly involved in their solution. II

SS 565   Make judgments on the judicial system in the United States using these criteria: (1) method of selecting the jury, (2) methods of selecting the judges, (3) use of bail for retaining suspects, and (4) past and present judicial decisions reported in mass media. VI

SS 570   Make judgments on the effectiveness of protection of individual rights in the United States. VI

SS 575   Make judgments on the effectiveness of provisions in our government that allow individuals to influence decisions. VI

SS 580   Show your understanding of cause and effect in political interaction by explaining the origins and results of a political event of your choice. II

SS 585   Show that you can discuss the democratic ideals expressed by 18th-century writers as they are implemented today in two countries. III

SS 590   Show that you can support or refute the value of contributions made by Roman law, Greek democracy, and Judeo-Christian ethics to the social-political structure of Western civilization. III

SS 595   Demonstrate your ability to combine concepts, principles, and generalizations by developing an outline for a national governmental structure that, in your opinion, is ideal. V

SS 600   By forming generalizations about a given world crisis, demonstrate your ability to perceive causes of international conflict. IV

SS 605   Demonstrate your ability to combine concepts, principles, and generalizations by developing a theory of political control over international conflicts which might be the basis for a world organization of nations. V

TERMINAL OBJECTIVES

SS 610   Develop guidelines for the foreign policy of an imaginary democratic country that provide for an effective leadership for world peace. Use these guidelines to evaluate given examples of United States foreign policy.   VI

SS 615   Show that you can reasonably predict the future of one of the following countries in the power structure of the world's nations: Soviet Union, Red China, any country in Southeast Asia.   III

SS 620   Make judgments on the philosophy of Marx as conceived in the U.S.S.R. and in Red China.   VI

SS 625   Make judgments on totalitarianism on the basis of effectiveness, efficiency, and freedom of individuals to make choices.   VI

GeOGraPHY

PRIMARY

SS 040   Show that you can locate places, climatic regions and physical features on maps and globes.   III

SS 045   Show that you can use map symbols and judge distances on a map.   III

SS 050   Show that you can relate physical features to climatic regions on maps and globes.   III

SS 055   Show your understanding of relationships between environmental resources and human activities in your community.   II

SS 060   Show your understanding of relationships between environmental resources and human activities in mountain regions.   II

TERMINAL OBJECTIVES

SS 065   Show your understanding of relationships between environmental resources and human activities in grassland areas.   II

SS 070   Show your understanding of relationships between environmental resources and human activities in desert communities.   II

SS 075   Show your understanding of relationships between environmental resources and human activities in arctic areas.   II

SS 080   Show your understanding of general effects of relationships between environmental resources and human activities.   II

INTERMEDIATE

SS 335   Show that you can use maps and globes to find information.   III

SS 340   Show your understanding of weather conditions and methods of predicting, measuring, and recording weather conditions.   II

SS 345   Show your understanding of climate conditions and their causes.   II

SS 350   Show your understanding of the influence of physical environment of people's lives.   II

SS 355   Show that you can use resource maps, globes, atlases, and related reference books to collect information about natural resources and human activities including agriculture and production.   III

SS 360   Show that you can use resources and references to plan a month-long trip for your family.   III

SS 365   Make a judgment of the effectiveness of an ecology program which is in progress or has been recently proposed.   VI

TERMINAL OBJECTIVES

SECONDARY

SS 630   Show that you can locate political features on maps and globes.   III

SS 635   Show that you can locate physical features on maps and globes.   III

SS 640   Show that you can locate climatic regions on maps and globes.   III

SS 645   Show that you can locate on maps and globes areas where natural and industrial goods are produced.   III

SS 650   Show that you can use political, physical, and climatic features of a given location to make reasonable predictions on one of the following: (1) agricultural production, (2) economic development, and (3) cultural identities of the population.   III

economics

PRIMARY

SS 085   Show that you know about basic human needs.   I

SS 090   Show your understanding of human dietary needs and of human activities concerned with meeting these needs.   II

SS 095   Show that you know about various aspects of food processing.   I

SS 100   Show that you know about various aspects of clothing and its production.   I

SS 105   Show your understanding of human need for shelter and special adaptations to various conditions.   II

SS 110   Show that you know about various aspects of building construction.   I

TERMINAL OBJECTIVES

SS 115 Show your understanding of some aspects of trading and of the use of money. II

SS 120 Show your understanding of community service work. II

SS 125 Show that you know about workers and occupations that affect you. I

SS 130 Show that you know about various aspects of merchandising. I

SS 135 Show that you can identify and use types of communication services. III

SS 140 Show that you know about types of transportation services. I

SS 145 Show that you know about various aspects of industrial production in factories. I

SS 150 Show that you know about various aspects of farm production. I

INTERMEDIATE

SS 370 Show that you can discuss the problems encountered in an economy when natural resources, human resources, and means of production are not all located in one place. III

SS 375 Show that you can use economics concepts and terms in discussing current events. III

SS 380 Show that you can discuss the features of an economy that place it within a particular economic category. III

SS 385 Show that you can use mathematic skills in solving personal economic problems. III

TERMINAL OBJECTIVES

SECONDARY

SS 655 Make judgments on steps for prevention or correction of a depression advocated by different political groups on the basis of their effect on (1) the economic health of the nation, and (2) the welfare of individuals.   VI

SS 660 Make judgments on three current proposals for solving the problems of poverty in the United States.   VI

SS 665 Show that you can discuss the economic problems and potentials of any area of your choice and can suggest a solution for each problem.   V

SS 670 Show that you can discuss the advantages and disadvantages of a completely free enterprise system, a controlled economy, and a mixed economy.   III

SS 675 Make judgments on taxes your parents pay in relation to these factors.   VI
1. The equity of the tax payments in relation to ability to pay
2. The equity of the tax in relation to equal responsibility in a democracy
3. The services provided by taxes through local, state, and federal government action

SS 680 Show that you can find solutions to personal economic problems.   III

PSYCHOLOGY and PHILOSOPHY

PRIMARY

SS 155 Show that you understand basic aspects of communication.   II

SS 160 Show that you can use problem-solving skills in situations involving personal problems.   III

SS 165 Show that you can make choices on the basis of needs, resources, and desires.   III

TERMINAL OBJECTIVES

INTERMEDIATE

SS 395   Show that you can recognize personal problems and apply problem-solving skills and human relations skills to their solution.   III

SS 400   Show that you understand the importance of interpersonal relationships in solving social problems.   II

SS 405   Demonstrate your ability to perceive problems of teenagers by analyzing specific problems on the basis of both experience and information.   IV

SS 410   Show your understanding of aspects of careers in the following occupational areas: industrial trade, business, commercial service, health service.   II

SS 415   Demonstrate your ability to combine concepts, principles, and generalizations by selecting at least two major world religions (not your own) and developing a project (report, diary, panorama, collage) that illustrates how the religions affect daily activities.   V

SS 420   Demonstrate your ability to combine concepts, principles, and generalizations by developing a set of social values based on information pertaining to a specific problem you have analyzed.   V

SECONDARY

SS 685   Show your understanding of aspects of careers in the following occupational areas: building trades, business, technical services, social services.   II

SS 690   Make judgments on two possible career choices for yourself. Use these criteria: (1) interest; (2) developed abilities scores; (3) performance in related objectives; (4) job potential; (5) salary potential and fringe benefits; (6) congruency with your value system.   VI

SS 695   Using your own set of social values as a basis for analysis, demonstrate your ability to perceive the difficulties individuals meet in living according to their values under

TERMINAL OBJECTIVES

the social controls imposed by their own community. Consider these problems: (1) the compromises an individual should or should not make in living in that community; (2) the impact the implementation of an individual's social values might have on his community; (3) the psychological problems for an individual who is forced to compromise his values.   IV

SS 700   Demonstrate your ability to combine concepts, principles, and generalizations by developing a list of criteria for selection of a religion most suitable for the individual.   V

SOCIAL STUDIES INQUIRY SKILLS

PRIMARY

SS 170   Show that you can make a list of questions to find out information.   III

SS 175   Show that you can use information to make a short simple report orally, in pictures, or in writing.   III

SS 180   Show that you can use maps and globes to locate places and to identify physical features, to judge distances, and to represent an area you know (your yard, neighborhood or classroom).   III

SS 185   Show that you understand the steps in problem solving and can apply them in dealing with your personal problems.   III

INTERMEDIATE

SS 425   Analyze statements on the basis of clarity, bias, assumptions, generalizations, and conclusions.   IV

SS 430   Demonstrate your skills in social studies research by choosing a topic, using appropriate sources of information, organizing the information and writing or presenting a report. Use a topic from any of the major social studies subjects.   III

SS 435   Demonstrate ability to plan a month-long trip for your family.   III

SECONDARY

SS 705   Demonstrate your ability to perceive the relevance of social science data to the topic being considered, to the authority of its source and its freedom from bias.   IV

SS 710   Demonstrate your ability to use information sources as required in social studies.   III

SS 712   Demonstrate your ability to present and support a hypothesis regarding an area of social studies. Your presentation may be written or oral and may take the form of a plan or a simulation model.   IV

SS 715   Demonstrate your ability to combine concepts, principles, and generalizations by using varied resource materials to develop a library research paper in which you present a hypothesis related to a social studies problem.   V

SS 720   Demonstrate your ability to make judgments regarding personal decisions based on reliable data.   VI

SS 725   Demonstrate your ability to use maps and globes as needed in social studies.   III

InDex

INDEX

INDEX

INDEX

INDEX

INDEX

INDEX

Irony, LA:86
Isolationism, SS:104
Isotopes, SC:57, 75
Isotopes, radioactive, SC:59
Italian unification, SS:100

Jefferson, Thomas, SS:91
Jobs, *see* Careers
Joints, SC:12
Judeo-Christian ethics, SS:99, 137
Judicial system, SS:92
Juvenile delinquency, SS:64

Kentucky, SS:17
Kerner Report, SS:84
Kinetic energy, SC:26, 27, 64, 67
Kinetic theory of gases, SC:67–68
King, Martin Luther, Jr., SS:84; LA:99
Koch, Robert, SC:50

Laboratory equipment, SC:81–82
Labor unions, SS:126, 127
Lamarck's theory of inheritance of acquired characteristics, SC:48
Language arts, intermediate level, LA:19–64
Language arts, primary level, LA:1–18
Language arts, secondary level, LA:65–108
Language development, LA:83
Laplander, SS:2, 8
Latin America, SS:35, 38, 114
Latin America, colonization of, SS:25
Latin America, exports, SS:53
Latin America, forms of government, SS:46
Latin America, social and economic problems, SS:36–38, 124
Latin American Indian culture, SS:35
Latin American revolutions, SS:37
Latitude, SS:50
Law of conservation of energy, SC:62, 67
Laws, *see* Politics and legislation
Laws of reflection, SC:69
League of Nations, SS:102, 106
Learning principles, LA:75
Least common multiple, MA:15
Legislative branch, SS:90
Legislative process, SS:92, 96

INDEX

INDEX

INDEX

INDEX

BeHavioral OBjectives

A Guide to Individualizing Learning

Text: Videocomp 9 point Roma with 10 point Roma Bold, display lines in 14 point Dimensia

Design and art: Steven Jacobs Design, Palo Alto, California

Editorial and production: Westinghouse Learning Press, Palo Alto, California

Composition, lithography, binding, packaging: Kingsport Press, Kingsport, Tennessee